Educating the Generations

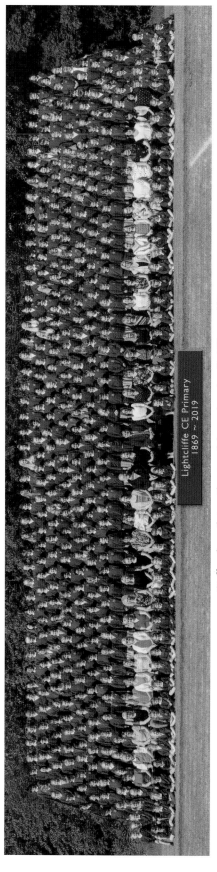

Staff and pupils together to celebrate the school's 150 years' history.
(Courtesy of H. Tempest Ltd)

Educating the Generations

Lightcliffe Church of
England School
1869 – 2019

John Brooke

Lightcliffe and District Local History Society

Published by Lightcliffe and District Local History Society
www.lightcliffehistory.org
Email: admin@lightcliffehistory.org.uk

ISBN: 978-1-9162983-0-9

Typeset in Garamond
Page layout by Highlight Type Bureau Ltd
Printed and bound by The Amadeus Press, West 26 Business Park,
Cleckheaton, BD19 4TQ

Cover designed by Steve Waddington, The Amadeus Press

Cover image courtesy of Chris Helme

Contents

For Geoffrey Gilder Hudson
1943-2012

**Geoff Hudson is seen here on the left, as we sign
copies of the second edition of 'The Story of a School'
in 1997.**

Foreword

My four-year-old grandson, George, started in the reception class at Lightcliffe School today. For months he's referred to it as 'My School'. I haven't said anything to him but, since 14 April, 1953, my first day in Mrs. Edwards's class, I've thought of it as my school. To my three children, who attended in the seventies and eighties, it is their school. And, of course, countless thousands of local children have, for the past 150 years, regarded the building at Knowle Top with similar proprietorial warmth.

John Brooke has a thorough knowledge of the development of education in England. In these pages he never loses sight of the wider picture, from before the passing of Forster's Education Act, through compulsory education for all, half-timers, the years of elementary education when most would stay in the one school until finding work at the age of 14, the eleven-plus, and the coming of comprehensive secondary education. However, the strength of this book, for me, lies as much in the attention to everyday detail, often through entries from log books.

We learn of pupil absences at times of haymaking and fruit-picking, the abandonment of slates in 1905, the arrival of evacuees in the two world wars. The installation of electric lighting in 1925 must have made life easier for staff, and I can only imagine the excitement in July 1942 when 'the wall separating the boys' and girls' playgrounds was taken down on the instructions of the managers'.

My memories of six years' gradual progression from that first day in 1953 to the top class are mostly affectionate ones. I remember the kindness of Mrs Edwards and Mrs Ward in the infants: storytime, under the weeping ash on sunny summer days (*Émile and the Detectives* a favourite), learning poems ('Oh, to be in England …') and bellowing rousing choruses of *Men of Harlech* and *Hearts of Oak*. The germination of lifelong enthusiasms. In the juniors were Miss Aspinall and Miss Sykes and the dry-humoured Harold Laycock, class teacher in my final year. I felt secure there.

It is startling to realise that my acquaintance with the school spans almost half of the 150 years of its existence. Inevitably, I see many changes. There are no gardening lessons, when we wore clogs left over from 'Dig for Victory' days. No inkwells, filled by monitors before school on Monday mornings. The air-raid shelters have gone. So has the morning playtime bottle of free milk. What remains is what's most important: the sense that here is a solid community, well grounded, well organised and ever caring, providing successive generations of local youngsters with an affinity that will last their whole lives.

As a social historian, John Brooke recognises the fundamental part Lightcliffe School has played in the history of our village. In *Educating the Generations* he conveys this understanding with clarity and perception.

Bob Horne
Chairman, Lightcliffe & District Local History Society
4 September, 2019.

Preface

It is fifty years since my friend Geoff Hudson and I collaborated on the first edition of *The Story of a School,* written to celebrate the school's centenary. This was followed in 1997 by a revised and updated edition. As the school celebrates its 150th year it is good that the local history society is publishing this further revision.

Both Geoff and I began our teaching careers at the school in the early 1960s and, although we moved on to other schools, Lightcliffe School would always remain part of our lives. The staff lists at the back of this book show that our wives also taught here although not, in my case, at the same time as me. Two of my sons, Matthew and Michael, also attended the school. Geoff died in 2012, so on this occasion I am the sole author, although some of his original writing survives here.

There is something special about this school. Perhaps it is that so many people currently living in the area have present or past links to it. Many of them will have attended the school or have parents, grandparents even great and great-great-grandparents who attended. It is still at the heart of the community with well over 400 pupils, many of whom are from those families that have long-standing connections to the school. Happily, it also retains its church foundation, established in 1869, and its links to St Matthew's church.

Its southern facade has remained virtually unchanged. The view from Wakefield Road that I saw when I stepped off the Yorkshire Woollen District 24 bus prior to my first teaching post interview all those years ago is still as it was. It was at that interview that I learned that Lightcliffe was, indeed, a special place. When asked by the then headteacher, George Armitage, if I played the piano, I offered the somewhat naive comment that I did, but with only one hand. He quickly informed me, virtually without altering his expression or moving his lips, that in Lightcliffe they had two-handed pianos!

I am conscious that although this is a history of Lightcliffe School there is much in it that is associated with my own career in education. I apologise, therefore, for the use of the occasional personal pronoun and for the number of times that I appear in some of the images. It is difficult to avoid both when I spent a total of almost twenty years, in two separate spells, at the school.

Finally a brief word about what I have tried to achieve here. This is not a full reworking of the previous editions, although a good deal of the text, albeit edited, remains. What I have tried to do is to make this more of a celebratory volume, with extra illustrations. The illustrations were picked from an enormous collection held by the school, and by others, and are very much an eclectic mix. Headteachers are covered where we have images, as are staff groups. It is disappointing that very few, if any, photographs of staff groups prior to 1967 exist (my guess is that they were not taken). This is also the case with class photographs where only pupils are shown. Some headteachers had a policy, certainly George Armitage had, of not including the staff member with the pupils. This I have found to be somewhat frustrating and I can imagine that readers will feel the same. It is so good to look back and see just how young (or old) our teachers were!

The class photographs have also been a source of mild irritation as in nearly every case all the pupils are unnamed. Attempting to identify each and everyone was, I regret to say, a step too far. It was decided, therefore, to name only those, if we knew them, who were referenced the text. I hope that you are still able to enjoy the images and possibly even recognise yourself!

As in 1969, and in 1997, I have received a good deal of help from many people for which I am most grateful. Charles Woodbridge, the headteacher, has been both enthusiastic and supportive. Nothing has been too much trouble to him as I have pestered him endlessly re the school records and access to the building. Helen Bell, the school business manager, has also been most agreeable and always found the time to be helpful. Former headteacher Tony Berwick has generously allowed me to use some of the information recorded during his time in office. Cath Macdonald, former deputy headteacher, willingly recalled events from the time that she worked with Tony, Charles and me.

Dorothy Barker, the secretary of Friends of St Matthew's Churchyard has researched the backgrounds of the early headteachers and this has been so useful in filling in the gaps re their careers. Lance and Irene Cook have been most supportive in letting me have further information about Lance's great-grandfather and former head teacher, William Cook. David Ellis kindly provided details about his great-uncle and former caretaker Francis Bradley. Brian and Patricia Barrand were happy to answer my questions relating to their experience during the war when Brian was here, initially, as a refugee from Alderney. Peter Foskett, the Leeds Diocesan Registrar, was helpful in forwarding copies of the title deeds and offering general advice. West Yorkshire Archive Service staff at Wakefield and Calderdale went out of their way to be helpful. Susan Thomis and Marjorie Middleton, the daughter of former headteacher Norman Lister, have helped to choose the photographs included here from the vast amount available. There was at times, almost inevitably, an element of random sampling in the final choices. Others, too numerous to mention individually, have provided snippets of information, photographs and documents. I hope that they will accept this general thank you.

Bob Horne, a good friend, and chairman of the Lightcliffe and District History Society, has helped in so many ways. I have regularly sought his wise counsel on matters relating to, for example, the text and the format, and this has always been so willingly given. More than that, though, he has cast his sharp eye over the whole work and sensitively pointed out my many initial errors. The production team at Amadeus have been available at every stage of the book's journey. David Crossland, the manager, has always found time to offer advice and Angela Lawless at Highlight Type Bureau has been equally friendly and helpful.

JMB
Lightcliffe
October 2019

Introduction

The first pupils were admitted to the Lightcliffe National Schools in February 1869. The buildings, which cost around £5,000, were generously paid for by Evan Charles Sutherland Walker who was, at the time, the occupant of Crow Nest mansion. Sutherland Walker also provided the four acres of land and the landscaping.

Until 1906, with the exception of a four-year break from 1894, the foundation building housed two separate schools. There was a boys' school in the western half and a girls' and infants' school in, respectively, the eastern half and central portion. There were residences at each end of the building for the master and mistress and these were occupied initially by John Otty Rusholme and Mary Lois Drake.

Until the 1944 Education Act, after which it became a primary school for children aged 4-11, Lightcliffe had been an elementary school for pupils up to the school leaving age of, by then, fourteen.

There have been four major phases of extensions to the original building along with a number of internal reconfigurations. The first development was in 1966 when a corridor, internal toilets, cloakrooms, storerooms, and both new headteacher's office and staffroom were added to the northern aspect. A second phase in 1973 saw the addition of a large hall and a two- classroom block.

In 1984 three further classrooms were added along with a large kitchen. In 1990, following the closure of Hipperholme Infants' School, a large block was added with provision specifically aimed at reception age children. Five years later a new entrance area was developed and later a new staffroom was created in the roof void of the central section. A further realignment of the visitors' entrance has taken place recently.

Despite all the extensions the immediate environs of the school have changed very little over the years. Some housing development that can be seen from the school has taken place and one such development is Park Close, built on the site of the railway goods yard. This closed in 1967, two years later than the passenger station, which closed in June 1965.

Chapter One

The Lightcliffe Schools are Built

In March 1866 the *Halifax Guardian* made the following plea, based on the apparently avid desire for learning by the people of Lightcliffe, that:

It is a matter of urgent necessity that more school accommodation should be provided

This was, of course, before William Edward Forster's 1870 Elementary Education Act and the establishment of school boards. Education was still, at the time, in the hands of the voluntary societies. In the Lightcliffe and Hipperholme area there were two modest elementary schools at Bramley Lane and at Coley, and a grammar school at Hipperholme, the foundation of which dates from 1648. The Bramley Lane School was established at the Lightcliffe Congregational Chapel by Titus Salt in 1846. It closed in 1879. The building itself had been superseded as a place of worship in 1871 when the fine building on Leeds Road was first used for worship. The original building continued as a Sunday School until 1892 when it was replaced by 'large and handsome' buildings that were erected alongside the church.

At Coley the Church School was established in 1845 and closed in 1875 when there were both management and financial problems. The vicar of Coley, William H Waun, had for 28 years been the sole manager of the school and had, 'again and again', endeavoured to persuade gentlemen who should be most interested in the management of schools, and the education of the working classes, to share the responsibility for those schools.

Provision was, therefore, limited and clearly wasn't available to all. For many their lot was still long hours in the mills, the factories and pits. Education still wasn't free and for the majority of poor children there was simply nothing at all. However, in Lightcliffe, one man particularly was aware of this and the school that we know today is his memorial. That man was Evan Charles Sutherland Walker and it was he, and he alone, who provided the land and built the schools with what, at the time, was a huge donation of £5000.

What was it, people must have wondered, that persuaded Sutherland Walker to approach the vicar of Lightcliffe with his generous proposal? Was it, as he indicated later, simply 'an honest desire to do good' or had it wider implications? He knew that a far-reaching Education Act was on its way and that local meetings to that effect had been held as early as 1850. On 4 May of that year the *Halifax Guardian* had reported that a meeting in Halifax, whilst giving due credit to the voluntary societies, had deemed it necessary that a 'system of national secular education be established, supported by local management and local votes'.

That gathering preceded the 1870 Education Act and board schools by twenty years. The practicality of these ideas was, however, being discussed and men of politics began to formulate plans for establishing state, non-denominational schools. It is more than probable that the augur of these 'religionless' schools prompted Sutherland Walker to initiate plans for the school. The act did not dismiss voluntary schools and where the local provision was adequate, or could be provided by the societies, a board and a local rate would not be imposed on the community.

Evan Charles Sutherland Walker
1835-1913

Evan Charles Sutherland Walker resided at Crow Nest, one of the largest houses in Lightcliffe. It was built for William Walker (1713-1786) in around 1778 to plans by Thomas Bradley that were a close copy of John Carr's Pye Nest in Halifax. So close, in fact, that Waterson and Meadows suggest that 'rarely can there have been such a blatant example of architectural plagiarism'. The entrance to the second drive and the lodge, to the west of St Matthew's Church, can be seen to this day although Crow Nest was demolished in the late 1950s. What a fine property it was with its 25-feet library, its 28 by 20 feet drawing room, 16 bedrooms, landscaped grounds, a well- stocked lake, vineries, pineries and a banana house. There was nothing more gratifying, said Horsfall Turner, than 'an hour's sojourn amongst the profusion of hot-house and other plants'.

Crow Nest: The home of Evan Charles Sutherland Walker.
(C D Helme collection)

Sutherland Walker's connection with Crow Nest began when his father, George Mackay Sutherland of Udale, on the Black Isle peninsula north of Inverness, was a captain with the 93rd Sutherland Highlanders billeted in Halifax. At a local ball George (1798-1847) met his future wife, Elizabeth Walker (1801-1844) of Cliffe Hill. They married at Lightcliffe in 1828. It is Elizabeth's sister Ann, though, who provides us with the direct link to the establishment of the school.

Evan Charles, who was born in 1835, had gained possession of Crow Nest from his aunt Ann Walker, the friend of Anne Lister. Ann had inherited the estate following the deaths of other family members, including Evan Charles's mother, her sister. Having no heir Ann proposed that, on her death, Evan Charles should inherit the estate. The terms of the agreement simply required him to add the Walker name to his Sutherland surname. This he did when Ann died in 1854 aged 50. He went on to marry Alice Sophia Tudor in 1859, and in1867 sold the property to Titus Salt who lived there until his death in 1876. Sutherland Walker's new home was Skibo Castle in Scotland where he lived until he sold the property to the Scottish born American industrialist Andrew Carnegie in 1898.

It was during his final two years in Lightcliffe that he set about building an elementary school for the area. Work began in1866 and those who attended St Matthew's Church on 14 April of that year were informed from the pulpit by the Archdeacon of Halifax, the Venerable Dr Charles Musgrave that:

It has ever been the reproach of friends of the church in this village that there was no school. This, however, is to be removed, for operations have already commenced towards the erection of a handsome block of buildings to consist of a boys' and a girls' school. with master's and mistress's houses. The school is near the station and will occupy an acre of ground ... The execution of the plans is entrusted to Mr Edgar Fletcher of White Hall. The cost of the whole will be defrayed by Evan Charles Sutherland Walker Esq. of Crow Nest who has also given the land.

The crest on the central section of the building facing Wakefield Road, on which the initials ECSW appear, records the date of this announcement and not the date of the schools' opening date. By the middle of the following year it appears that the external structure was complete to the satisfaction of both Sutherland Walker and the man responsible for the fine design, his agent John Smith. Smith had worked for Sutherland Walker since moving from Scotland some 24 years earlier. He died in September 1882 aged 71 and is buried in Lightcliffe churchyard. He had, noted the *Halifax Courier*, possessed 'some skill as a draughtsman, and in the general construction of buildings had sought to apply modern appliances'.

The crest on the central section of the foundation building. Along with the initials ECSW it bears the date that the school was originally planned to open.

In the October of 1867 churchgoers heard again from the Venerable Musgrave when it was announced that:

Now through the munificence of Evan Charles Sutherland Walker ... we have schools erected that are without rival in this parish. It is hoped that energetic steps will be taken to encourage the attendance of children. [Attendance at school was still not compulsory at the time.]

The church referred to on a number of occasions above was the fine Georgian building opposite the Sun Inn of which only the tower remains. It was built in 1775 with the help of William Walker of Crow Nest. Ann Walker is buried there. The present church, opened in 1875, was the gift of the Foster family of Cliffe Hill.

By January 1868 the schools were still unoccupied and would be for a further twelve months. In a newspaper article relating to the departure of the Bramley Lane school's headmaster, there was a rather sardonic reference in the local papers to the unoccupied new school building. 'New schools have been erected', it was noted, 'but to what purpose they are to be appropriated is not known nor when they are to be opened'.

Progress was being made, however, and by September the title deeds had been drawn up and handed to the four trustees: the Vicar of Halifax, the Vicar of Lightcliffe and the two churchwardens. The salient points of the deed are as follows:

I Evan Charles Sutherland Walker, the owner of the unsold portions of the Crow Nest Estates ... do hereby freely and voluntarily and without any valuable consideration grant and convey to the Venerable Charles Musgrave and the Reverend William Gurney, John Henry Wurtzburg and Benjamin Skelton Ward ... all the plot, piece or parcel of land situate in Lightcliffe commonly known as the Five Days' Work and the Knoll....buildings, recently erected upon the said plot of land to permit the said premises to be forever hereafter appropriated ... for schools and also the residences of the schoolmasters and schoolmistress of the said schools ... to be always in union with the National Society for promoting the education of the poor in the principles of the Church of England.

As the title deeds were handed over to the trustees, Sutherland Walker generously gave a further sum, £80 19s 3d, to enhance the building and the grounds. Thomas Pyrah of Hipperholme was employed to paint the schools and Abraham Fairburn of Wyke to landscape the grounds. The work was to be supervised by the assistant curate, the Reverend J Wynne.

As indicated in the title deed the schools were given the prefix National. The term originated from the early nineteenth century, and was closely associated with Dr Andrew Bell an Anglican clergyman. He had begun around that time, along with the Quaker Joseph Lancaster, to utilise a system of cheap education known as the monitorial system. Pupils were taught in a one-room school at Borough Road, London, by other pupils (monitors) who had received their instruction from the school's only master. When the two men split, Lancaster's schools flourished under the auspices of 'The British and Foreign Bible Society' and were supported by

Walker

—— and ——

The Archdeacon of Craven

Evan Charles Sutherland Walker the Owner of the unsold portion of The Crow Nest Estates situate in the West Riding of the County of York and of No 2 Grosvenor Crescent in the Parish of Saint George Hanover Square in the County of Middlesex Esquire under the authority of an Act passed in the fifth year of the reign of Her present Majesty Queen Victoria intituled An Act for affording further facilities for the conveyance and endowment of Sites for Schools DO nearly freely and voluntarily and without any valuable consideration grant and convey to The Venerable Charles Musgrave Doctor in Divinity Archdeacon of the Archdeaconry of Craven in the said County of York and Vicar of Halifax in the same County The Reverend William Gurney Clerk Master of Arts Vicar of Lightcliffe in the said Parish of Halifax and John Henry Wurtzburg of No 2 Walshaw Crescent in Hipperholme in the said Parish of Halifax Merchant and Benjamin Mellor Maud of Sunside in Lightcliffe aforesaid Gentleman the Churchwardens for the time present of the Chapelry or Church commonly called Saint Matthew situate in Lightcliffe in the Parish of Halifax and Riding aforesaid ALL that plot piece or parcel of land or ground situate in Lightcliffe in the said Parish of Halifax as the same is now marked and set out off and from two certain closes pieces or parcels of land or ground called or commonly known by the several names of The Five Days Work and The Knoll heretofore part of the Lidgate Estate and which said plot piece or parcel of land or ground is bounded on the north by a footway leading from Smawley Lane into the Lidgate Estate on the south by the Halifax and Wakefield Turnpike Road on the east by Smawley Lane and on the west by Lots 236, 237 and 238 on the Sale plan of the Crow Nest Estates contains in the whole by admeasurement four acres one rood and thirty eight perches or thereabouts and is with its abuttals and boundaries more particularly delineated and described in the plan drawn in the margin of the first skin of these presents and is therein coloured blue and also all and every the erections buildings or tenements recently erected upon the said plot piece or parcel of land or ground or some part thereof by me the said Evan Charles Sutherland Walker and consisting of a School house and Teachers house with the outbuildings tenements and appurts thereto belonging together with all and singular the rights members and appurts to the said plot piece or parcel of land or ground erections buildings or tenements hereditaments and premises belonging or in anywise appertaining Excepting Nevertheless and reserving hereout the Lead water main running from the water drift in Lot 232 on the Sale plan of the Crow Nest Estates to Lot 81 on the same which main shall belong to the purchaser

The Title Deed (section of)
(Courtesy of Leeds Diocesan Registry)

5

nonconformists. (The school at Bramley Lane was often referred to as a British School). Bell's efforts resulted in the formation of the National Society in 1811 and, in turn, National Schools.

All was just about ready then for the opening of the new National Schools early in the following year, and the key appointments of the master and the mistress.

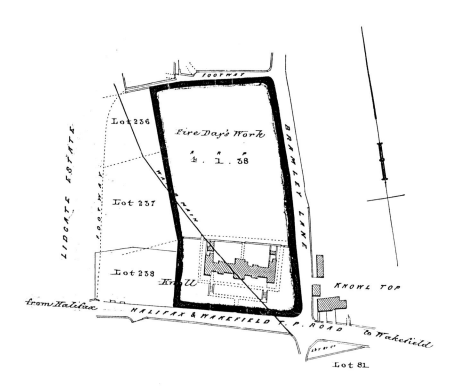

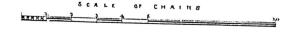

The 'Five Days' Work'
This comprised four acres, one rood and 38 perches.
Note that Bramley Lane then extended to what is now Knowle Top Road.
(Courtesy of Leeds Diocesan Registry)

Chapter Two

The Opening of the Schools

It appears that the first pupils attended Mr Sutherland Walker's fine new school on 1 February 1869 but prior to that there was an opening ceremony on Tuesday 12 January to celebrate formally the new school. However, even before the formal opening local people had gained a good deal of information about the building from the columns of the local papers. The *Halifax Guardian* of 16 January 1869 described the building in felicitous terms:

The building in Elizabethan architecture with step gables, is commodious internally, and very handsome in the exterior appearance, being built of dressed stone.

The southern facade, of what is now often referred to as the foundation building is still, more or less, as it looked when the schools opened. Today the building is a little more concealed, the dressed stone somewhat darker but those passing the school on Wakefield Road see, with the exception of the missing weather vane, just what passers-by saw all those years ago.

We read more about the school in the paper's detailed description. The front part of the extensive grounds was 'beautifully laid out' and the whole length of the building formed ' a raised terrace with asphalted walks'. To the rear there was ample yard space and a three- acre field. There were 'excellent dwellings' for the master and mistress and accommodation *for 600 children.* (my italics)

The boys' school occupied the western section, the girls' school the eastern portion of identical size to the boys' accommodation, with the central section reserved for the infants. The large rooms which formed the two schools were partitioned in 1905. Many readers will remember the folding screens that were only replaced in 1966. There were fireplaces in all the rooms. The master's house was at the western end of the boys' school with the mistress's at the eastern (Knowle Top) end. The master's house was subsumed into the main school in 1927 but the mistress's house lived on as the caretaker's house long after the mistress no longer lived there. It has within the past few years been used by the 'Out of School Club'.

Despite the many alterations and improvements a 'peculiarity' noted at the time can still be made out to this day, but only just, that 'the girls' and infants school formed a letter 'T' with the infants' section 18 inches higher. The rooms were separate but could be converted into a large space by the folding back of the screen that was in place up to 1996. The space created was used for functions, such as the opening ceremony, and for productions by the pupils and other bodies.

The Opening Ceremony

This event that had, it appears, been looked forward to for many months was celebrated on Tuesday evening 12 January 1869. Despite the cold weather and the darkness the people of Lightcliffe and district, young and old, rich and poor turned out in large numbers to witness the proceedings. Perhaps many arrived at the railway station that had opened in 1850 or travelled in their private carriages. The local people would have walked to the school.

The evening began with a celebration tea which 600 people enjoyed including, reported the *Halifax Guardian,* several gentry. Many of the trays of food were gifts of the ladies of the district who also, no doubt, were responsible for the 'tasteful decorations' which were 'evergreens in various devices'.

The tea was followed by musical entertainment interspersed with addresses. The music, songs and glees were provided by Abraham Foster Esq and Mrs Foster of Northowram Hall, Jonas Foster Esq of Cliffe Hill and others. The Lightcliffe Church choir was augmented by singers from Halifax Parish Church. All the items were apparently well rendered although, at times, the choirboys' voices seemed, it was recorded, to be 'rather higher pitch than the pianoforte'.

The opening address was by the curate, in the absence of the vicar who was attending a sick person. He began by congratulating all on the beautiful buildings. There were, he said, no schools in the parish which combine so many advantages and it was 'nonsense' that some people thought that they were too big. The bigger they were the healthier they would be. He hoped that parents would do their part in sending the children to school and promised that the managers would do their duty. The school would, he hoped, teach them something that when they grew up would make them better men and women, 'mentally, socially, morally and religiously'.

The gathering then heard form the Vicar of Coley, who was welcomed with rounds of applause as he had just recovered from an illness lasting three years. About the school he would make two remarks. He hoped that they would be placed under Government inspection. He thought that some people might find it unpleasant having people finding fault 'with everything and everybody as was often the case, but nevertheless it would act as a spur'.

His second remark concerned the playground [the field]. He hoped that this would not only be used by the school children, but opened as a cricket ground for the young men of the neighbourhood then 'many a summer evening might be spent in innocent recreation which might otherwise be spent in the beer houses'.

This was followed by the presentation of the following address to Sutherland Walker. This had been 'specially prepared and beautifully executed' and written on parchment.

ENROLMENT NUMBER.	DATE OF ADMISSION. D.	M.	Y.	CHILD'S NAME. (Surname first.)	DATE OF BIRTH. D.	M.	Y.	PARENT'S CHRISTIAN NAME.	RESIDENCE.
1	11	4	92	Jagger George	3	9	85	Charles	Whitehall
2	11	4	92	Bradley John Ed.	12	6	86	George	Hill Top.
3	11	4	92	Lister Reginald	27	4	86	Teaver	Town Gate
4	12	4	93	Sucksmith John	24	11	86	William	Hill Top. Li'cliffe
5	12	4	93	Roper John	7	5	86	Thomas	Bracken Road.
6	2	3	94	Wilkinson Edgar	17	7	86	Hartley	Hill Top.
7	12	4	93	Hoyle Leonard	29	9	86	Charles H.	Gomersall Buildg
8	12	4	93	Butterfield Percy	11	10	86	John	Lydgate
9	12	4	93	Nichol Harry	8	9	86	Abraham	Whitehall
10	12	4	93	Robinson Joe	14	8	86	Henry	Prospect Terrace.
11	12	4	93	McKowen George E.	19	11	86	James	Dove House Cottage
12	4	12	93	Longbottom Percy	3	3	87	Thomas	Park View Terrace
13	27	8	94	Taylor Albert	22	4	86	Thomas	Gomersall's Bldgs
14	29	4	95	Womersley Robert	9	10	85	Jane	Spring Cottage. Li'cl.
15	20	4	94	Newsome Charles	31	3	87	Charles	Whitehall
16	20	4	94	Wakefield Ernest	26	11	87	Aurelius	Horton Terrace
17	20	4	94	Travis John	9	11	87	John	Lees Buildings.
18	20	4	94	Dove John	3	8	87	Daniel	Lane End Terrace
19	20	4	94	Wilkinson George	26	6	87	Fred	Whitehall. Hip.
20	20	4	94	Schofield Arnold	8	1	87	Arthur	Dove Cottages
21	20	4	94	Sharp Harold	23	10	86	Joseph	Broad Oak
22	20	4	94	Whiteley Arthur	2	8	86	John	Beaconsfield's Terrace
23	20	4	94	Craighill Thomas	19	11	87	Jonathan	Horton Terrace
24	20	4	94	Midgley Lewis	11	2	88	Arthur	North View L'cliffe
25	20	4	94	Bottomley Harry	21	10	87	Allan	Bracken Farm. Hip.
26	20	4	94	Hollings Leonard	30	9	87	Benjamin	Lydgate
27	20	4	94	Booth Fred	28	4	87	James	Ripley St.
28	23	4	94	Lee Wallace	25	11	86	Alfred	Lees Buildings.
29	4	6	94	Crabtree Abram	6	2	85	Abraham	Hoyle Farm Lcliffe
30	24	8	96	Greenwood John	3	8	86	Heaton Horsfall	Westend Farm
31	24	8	96	Rothery Harry	5	11	87	Herbert	Beaconsfield Terr

The first page of the earliest admission register to hand
This shows pupils admitted in the 1890s

The trustees and managers, on behalf of the church and themselves, desire to express their high sense of Mr Walker's liberality in providing such a handsome and commodious building for the religious, moral and intellectual training of the labouring classes amongst them. They trusted that the school would prove a blessing not only to the present, but to future generations; and they felt persuaded that the only compensation Mr Walker desired was that those who attended week after week might receive such instruction as shall fit them for the discharge of this life and for happiness and enjoyment in the life to come ... Dated Lightcliffe 12 January, 1869

Sutherland Walker then stood to speak and was greeted, reported the weekly *Halifax Courier* a few days later, with 'great cheering and applause repeated again and again'. He made a number of key points after indicating just how grateful he was for the address which he received with 'more pleasure than anything else he had ever had'. He hoped people would take an interest in the school and parents would not only send their children to the school but encourage them to learn whilst there. He believed that they were on the verge of great changes in education but hoped that a compulsory system that had been talked of would be rejected. It would, he believed, 'cause great discord in every place'.

He then received loud applause when he stated that no child would be compelled to learn the catechism. Perhaps he was aware that many who were likely to attend were not members of the Anglican Church, and was to be a school for all. He hoped that the school would be placed on as liberal a footing as possible with people having a say through the churchwardens. He hoped too that people would take an interest in the reading rooms (the small rooms at either end) and the playgrounds which were for young and old. Finally, when referring to the buildings, he modestly said that 'I can truly say that they are not for any personal glorification, but for an honest desire to do good'.

Further speeches followed, including one by W Ripley MP, who said there was no fear for the future when he looked at the smiling faces present. Those who were not present would soon, no doubt, hear about Mr Sutherland Walker's new school.

Although the schools had now been officially declared open a few weeks elapsed before the first scholars attended. The announcement that the people had been waiting for came on Sunday 31 January when the school had been used for public worship. Those present heard that the schools were now open for the reception of children and that John Otty Rusholme and Mary Lois Drake had been appointed master and mistress. It appears that some children attended the following day but precise records are scant. The first clear indication of children attending appeared in the *Halifax Guardian* on 10 April 1869 which stated that:

Lightcliffe National Schools, which were opened two months ago, under the charge of a certificated master and mistress, have already more than 120 children on their books...it appears that the parents of Lightcliffe appreciate the schools.

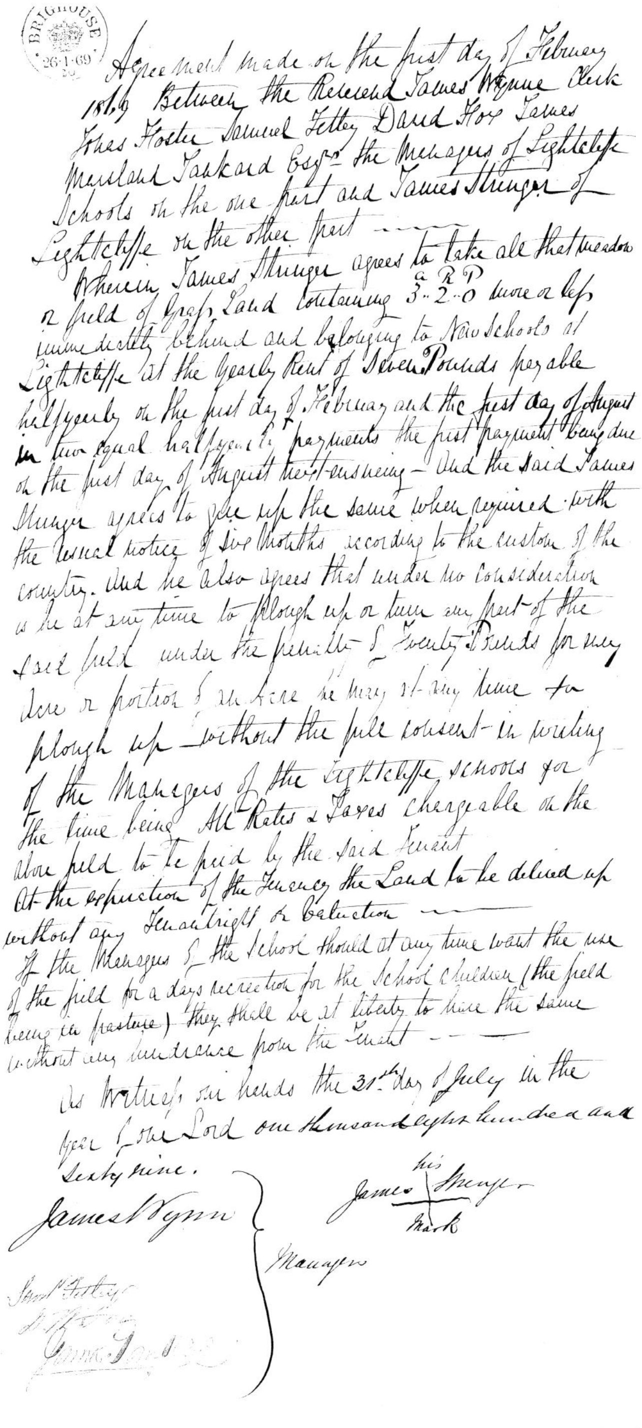

Agreement made on the first day of February 1869 Between the Reverend James Wynne Clerk John Foster Samuel Fetley David Fox James Marsland Tankard Esqrs the Managers of Lightcliffe Schools on the one part and James Stringer of Lightcliffe on the other part

Wherein James Stringer agrees to take all that meadow or field of Grass Land containing 3..2..0 more or less immediately behind and belonging to New Schools at Lightcliffe at the Yearly Rent of Seven Pounds payable half yearly on the first day of February and the first day of August in two equal half yearly payments the first payment being due on the first day of August next ensuing — And the said James Stringer agrees to give up the same when required with the usual notice of two months according to the custom of the country. And he also agrees that under no consideration is he at any time to plough up or turn any part of the said field under the penalty of Twenty Pounds for any acre or portion of an acre he may at any time so plough up without the full consent in writing of the Managers of the Lightcliffe schools for the time being All Rates & Taxes chargeable on the above field to be paid by the said Tenant At the expiration of the Tenancy the Land to be delived up without any Tenantright or Valuation —

If the Managers of the School should at any time want the use of the field for a days recreation for the School children (the field being in pasture) they shall be at liberty to have the same without any hindrance from the Tenant ———

As Witness our hands the 31st day of July in the year of our Lord one thousand eight hundred and Sixty nine.

James Wynn }

Saml Fetley
J. Foster
James Fox
} Managers

James   his   Stringer
         ✕
        mark

In 1869 James Stringer rented the land to the north of the school.
Readers will note that James was unable to write his name, as he has indicated his acceptance
of the agreement by simply making his mark.
(West Yorkshire Archives, Wakefield. Ref. WDP47/Box11)

11

The key appointments of the schools' first master and mistress appear to have been made shortly after the opening ceremony. John Otty Rusholme, the head of the boys' school was born in Hull in 1836. By 1861 he was a National School teacher in Harborne Staffordshire. He remained at Lightcliffe until 1873 when he returned to Hull. He died there in 1885 aged 49. Mary Drake was born in Wyke in 1846 and died in 1882 when still head of the girls' school. The 1881 census returns show her living at the school house with her parents and younger sisters Leah who was a schoolmistress, and Elizabeth, who was a music teacher.

This indicates, of course, that Mary was no more than 23 years old when she was appointed. She would, almost certainly, have been the only qualified (certificated) teacher for the girls and infants. She was paid £40 a year whereas the master, John Rusholme received £80. Records show, however, that by 1876 her salary had been raised to £60. The master's remained at £80.

The only guide to life in the school during the first year are the various amounts austerely recorded in the cash register. The first item is the gift from Sutherland Walker, already referred to, to help the schools on their way. Further donations followed in September when W H Ripley and Jonas Foster each gave £5, and the Hipperholme Local Board £6. A Government grant of £53 11s 6d is recorded the following year. The first income from 'school pence' was recorded on 30 April. The girls had paid £4 3s 5d and the boys £8 1s 6d. The children paid, it appears, a penny or two pence a week. There were payments to trades people such as Edwin Oates who received 5s 6d for window cleaning, and the gas bill was £3 7s for six months.

Chapter Three

The Schools Become Established
1870-1906

By 1870 there were approximately 200 children on the schools' registers. Many children in the area were, though, still not attending school. Many were still working, many of tender years, as it was not until 1876 that the employment of children under ten was forbidden.

The problem of insufficient education nationally was, up to a point, remedied by the 1870 Forster Act although it was still not compulsory or free. Compulsory education, up to the age of ten, (it was raised to eleven in 1893 and to twelve in 1899) came about with Anthony Mundella's Act of 1880.

William Edward Forster was a Bradford MP, a prosperous woollen manufacturer, a Quaker and a radical. He had married the daughter of Dr Thomas Arnold, the historian and head of Rugby School. The chief outcome of the act was that education was to be provided for all who wanted it. School boards were to be established where voluntary schools were insufficient. If the latter could show that that the education that they were providing was 'sufficient, efficient and suitable' then they could remain the sole providers. Locally the development of education followed the national pattern with the voluntary societies determined to build more schools.

In 1872 a Church School was established at Clifton; Rastrick St John's School was built in 1874, the two St Andrew's Schools in Brighouse in 1881, St James's in Brighouse in 1884 and Hipperholme Infants' School in 1885. A school board was formed in Rastrick in 1881. Fees (school pence) were abolished in both Board and Voluntary schools in 1891. School boards were replaced in 1902, following the Balfour Education Act, by 328 local education authorities, to work with the National Board of Education.

John Rusholme and Mary Drake were, as we have heard, leading the schools until 1873 when the former was replaced by William Cook. Prior to coming to Lightcliffe William Cook, who was born in Leeds in 1842, had worked in Lincolnshire and Old Windsor. He served Lightcliffe Boys' School until his premature death from 'bronchitis and weak action of the heart' on 5 November 1890. Boys from the school joined the funeral procession from the school house to the service in the old church, where he had been organist, prior to burial in the churchyard. He had, indicated the parish magazine of the time, 'possessed one of those genial natures which win the esteem and regard of everyone'. The family not only had the trauma of his death to

**William Cook. Headteacher of the boys' school
1893-1890**
(Lance and Irene Cook collection)

cope with but also had to move house. Two of the children, Hilda, aged nine, and Dorothy, five were still at school and there is a record of them leaving on 12 December 1890. There were also four older daughters and a son in the family. By 1881 they had moved to Leeds. When his wife Christiana died she was buried alongside her husband back in Lightcliffe.

The 1891 census shows Christiana and her family of six daughters and two sons living in West Leeds. Three of the daughters are listed as Elementary Schoolteachers and one of those was Dorothy who went on to be head of a number of infant schools in Leeds. Some time after that fateful day in 1890 it was she who wrote a detailed account of what she remembered of her time in Lightcliffe. This document is still to hand and it makes fascinating, but also poignant, reading:

Early Years at Lightcliffe

I was born on the 30th August 1885 at Lightcliffe, a village three miles from Halifax. My father was schoolmaster there and we lived in the school-house which was part of the main building. We had a very large garden and we played in it every evening in summer and all through the holidays ... One of my earliest recollections was that of being carried to the top of the wide staircase on Christmas morning to hear the choirboys sing the lovely carols. After singing my mother gave them Christmas cake and ginger wine ... Then came the great tragedy in our lives, when in November 1890, we were suddenly left fatherless ... It meant that the happy days in the big garden were at an end and a new life to be faced in the big city of Leeds ...

William Cook's death, after he had established a fine reputation, would have been a great tragedy also for the school and the community. Records show just how much progress the school was continuing to make during his time in charge. In 1885, for example, he would have been pleased to receive the following report from Her Majesty's Inspectors (HMI):

The instruction of the boys is carried out with unmistakable perseverance and earnestness on the part of Mr Cook. Much of the work is creditably done and what is amiss seems only to be due to carelessness and inattention.

The previous year there had been a favourable report and a generous grant, and the *Halifax Guardian* reported that 'the work of the school is always of a most satisfactory character'. This continued and just before William Cook's death the June 1890 parish magazine reported that:

The day schools continue to give great satisfaction to the managers, subscribers and parents. To get praise from an inspector like Mr Pole [Mark Pole, HMI living in Beech Road, Sowerby Bridge] *is not easy - we should greatly like the opportunity to cross-examine that gentleman on some of his own questions. . . .One of the managers will be glad to conduct parents or friends of the children through the school. They are extremely well worth a visit.*

Regular reports were an important aspect of school life and included attendance records and examination results part of the process by which annual grants were awarded. The basis of these grants had, though, changed radically seven years before the Lightcliffe schools opened. In 1862 Robert Lowe, vice-president of the Privy Council on Education introduced a system known as 'payment by results'. This was one outcome of the Newcastle Commission of 1858 which was set up to enquire into 'the present state of popular education'. The school received 6s 6d for satisfactory performance for infants, and 12 shillings for older children. There were penalties for both unsatisfactory results and attendance. Those not attending were eagerly sought and school boards, particularly, had their own 'board men', a term that lingered into the twentieth century long after grants depended on attendance.

Lowe's policy was not welcomed by those with enlightened minds as it meant an end to any attempt to teach outside the 'three Rs'. Children advanced through standards and often brighter children were held back or those less able were coerced, sometimes physically, to reach the required standard. (Each of the standards had a definite course of study and the standard was the level that the average child was expected to have reached by the end of a year's work. Pupils entered standard one at the age of about six.) Matthew Arnold, poet, enlightened school inspector and the brother-in-law of WE Forster, called it a game of 'mechanical contrivance' in which children were 'forcibly fed semi-digested facts'. The system continued for 28 years but left its mark for much longer.

At the girls' school during this period the first change of mistress had, as indicated, occurred later than at the boys. That was in 1882 when Mary Drake died aged 37, from causes associated with an underlying heart condition, and Mary Elizabeth Fairbrother was appointed. Little is known of Miss Fairbrother who was born in Manchester in 1853. She left the school and, it appears, the profession in 1887. In 1891 she was a draper living in Gorton, Manchester, and ten years later in Eccles. She retired to Morecambe where in 1911 we find her living with a servant, and supported by 'private means'. Her signature on the census return of that year confirms her identity, as it matches that which she added to school examination documents.

Mary Fairbrother was succeeded by Mary Clubbs, who was born in Longtown, Cumberland in 1860/1. She received a salary of £25 a quarter, a 'grant bonus' of £5, £3 for tuition of pupil-teachers and £7 voted by the managers. The pupil-teacher system was introduced in 1846 when certain schools were selected as training

EDUCATION DEPARTMENT.

Form No. 61.

F.&T. 10,000 6-79
[6-43-10]

To be filed in the School Portfolio when returned by the Inspector.

(To be filled up and to be ready on the day fixed for the Examination.)

NEW CODE.

DUPLICATE EXAMINATION SCHEDULE.

Lightcliffe Church _____ School.

Yorkshire _____ County.

LIST OF SCHOLARS on whose Account a Grant is claimed for the Year ended
October 31st, 18 79 , *(last day of month, Article 13.)*

N.B.—This Schedule must be filled up as an *exact* duplicate of the Examination Schedule furnished to the Inspector. If this duplicate is properly filled up and presented to the Inspector with the other, it will be returned to the Managers marked with the *failures* in column III., with the *passes* in column IV., and with an authority to the Teacher to issue the Certificates required by Labour Acts.

The Department does not undertake to supply the information otherwise than by means of these Duplicate Schedules, filled up and furnished to the Inspector at the proper time.

This Duplicate Schedule must be produced to the Inspector when he visits the School the following year, as his authority for the application of Art. 29 (*b*). He will not re-examine Scholars in the same Standard unless this Schedule is produced to him.

Certificate to be signed by the Teacher and countersigned by one of the Managers.

I certify that this Duplicate Schedule has been carefully verified with the original, and that, so far as regards Columns I., II., V., *Va.* and IX., it is an exact transcript of the same.

Signed *Mary Lois Drake* (Teacher)

this *5* day of *November* 18 79 .

Countersigned *George Bagot*

on behalf of the Managers.

Number	NAME	Examined and passed in* Reading	Writing	Arithmetic	Specific Subjects No. I. No. of Subject	Stage	Passed	No. II. No. of Subject	Stage	Passed	No. III. ex Stand. VI. only No. of Subject	Stage	Passed	Number of attendances in the year	See direction No. 2 on Exam. Sched.	Age (on LAST birthday)	Date of Admission to this School Year	Month	Under what class of school first began with lowest LAST ex-amined	NOW to be ex-amined	Under what Standard (I., II., &c.)
1	Amelia Pullen													406	9	75	2	5	No		I
2	Sarah Preson													270	7	77	9	"	"		"
3	Ada Hepworth													300	9	77	12	"	"		"
4	Annie Whitehead													373	8	77	12	"	"		"
5	E.A. Sharpe													314	9	77	12	"	"		"
6	Fr. Wright													284	7	77	11	"	"		"
7	Cressy Cook													303	7	75	3	"	"		"
8	Emma Stringer													366	7	75	6	"	"		"

* A cypher indicates *failure*. A cross or a blank indicates *pass*. Strike out the names of all children not actually examined.

The front page of an examination schedule.
This was completed by Lois Drake in 1879. All the girls shown here passed the tests but that was not the case on the pages that followed when a zero mark was recorded against a pupil's name.

grounds for apprentices who began at the age of 13. If they subsequently went to college they were recognised as 'certificated teachers'. They were rigorously tested and inspected annually. Mary Clubbs left the school in 1891 to become the wife of William Cook's successor John Robert Markham. Her resignation was, noted the July church magazine, deeply regretted by the managers, friends and supporters of the day schools as during her time as mistress of the girls' and infants' school she had 'worked up the school to a high standard of efficiency'. Tone, discipline and results alike had been excellent. The married couple had a son Leslie, born in September 1892, who was admitted to the school in April 1896, and a few years later a daughter Gwendoline was born. Mary Clubbs's successor was Janet Berry, who commenced duties as head of the Girls' School on 2 September 1891. Little did she know at the time what, initially, a short tenure it would be.

Janet was a local girl and one of the first pupils to attend the school. On the examination and attendance schedule for 1877, when 13 years old, she is recorded by Mary Drake as being admitted in February, 1869. She remained at the school as a pupil-teacher (there is a record of her earning £1 5s a quarter in May 1878) until leaving for Oxford Diocesan Training College. After teaching initially in Clapham Park, London she was appointed to succeed Mary Clubbs in 1891. She left the school when the amalgamation was effected three years later. We are able to have an insight into her experience when the schools amalgamated in a letter that she wrote to the managers' treasurer, Colin Johnson, in 1948 when the school was seeking to retain its voluntary status. 'The schools were so short of money', she recalled, 'that they were mixed and I left to teach in Czechoslovakia'. As we shall hear the amalgamated status was scrapped in 1898 and Janet Berry returned to the school as head of the girls' school as, she recorded many years later, 'successor to herself'!

The letter written by Janet Berry in 1948

17

A brief spell as a mixed school: 1894-8

Robert Markham was initially head of the boys' school and, from 1894-98, the mixed school following the decision to amalgamate the two schools. The change was brought about by 'those in higher authority' to lessen the expenses of working and to satisfy other requirements'.

The mixed school had opened on 20 August 1894 and Robert Markham observed in the log book at the time that, 'After the holidays the usual poor attendance has been very marked'. He may not have realised at the time but one of the contributing factors to this poor attendance may have been the amalgamation of the schools. Ethel Womersley, then a pupil at the school and a lady we shall hear more about in due course, remembered well in 1969 that 'mother said that she hadn't to be with the boys'.

Epidemics, such as scarlet fever in 1885 when the schools had to close, and inclement weather were also the cause of poor attendance. A typical entry in the logbooks is 'dark and raining—attendance deplorable'. This was very much the case in 1895 when the weather was unusually severe. During this time meals were provided for the pupils—perhaps as a way of ensuring their attendance. Robert Markham recorded on 8 February that he 'commenced giving 50 of the poorer children soup dinners as many of their fathers have not been able to work owing to the arctic conditions'.

Robert Markham now had male and female staff to assist him. There were two certificated assistants A. Ainsworth and Miss H Tomlinson (who was assisted by a monitor Mary Hey), and Misses Binns and Bairstow, assisted by pupil-teacher Thomas Hey. Two pupil-teachers Annie Oakes and a Miss Aspinall shared responsibility for Standard one.

Robert Markham left the school at Easter 1898 to become head of a school at Colney Heath in Hertfordshire. It is believed that he died in York in 1934. The parish magazine at the time of his departure from Lightcliffe noted that;

Mr Markham will relinquish his duties as Head Master in a short time, to the regret of many friends in the district. The Head Mastership has been held by him for eight years and he has generally obtained an excellent grant at the yearly examination. This reflects great credit on the school and more especially Mr Markham and the assistant teacher ... wherever Mr Markham finds his sphere of labour, our good wishes will follow both himself and his family for their future success and prosperity.

There was also a presentation to Robert Markham reported in the *Halifax Guardian*, as a mark of respect to which he is held by a large number of residents of the district.

Two separate schools again

Robert Markham's departure coincided with the return to two separate schools. He was replaced as head of the re-established boys' school by George Hague who began teaching in Leeds in 1886 and was, immediately prior to his appointment at

Lightcliffe, a lecturer at the Leeds Pupil-Teachers' Central Classes Institution. The parish magazine reported that George Hague came to the school with the 'highest credentials' and had had a 'most brilliant career in some of the best schools under the Leeds School Board'. He was chosen from a field of 'between 100 and 200 applicants'. So when the two separate school were reinstated the headteachers were George Hague and Janet Berry. On 7 May 1898 the *Halifax Guardian* hoped 'that the new arrangement would greatly increase the efficiency of the school'. Janet Berry's return was clearly popular and she would, reported the parish magazine of the time, 'be welcomed back to Lightcliffe by a large circle of friends and we feel confident ... that the Girls' School will soon become one of the best in the district'. The arrangements did not last long however for, as we shall hear, by 1906, following a decision by the West Riding County Council, there was again just one school.

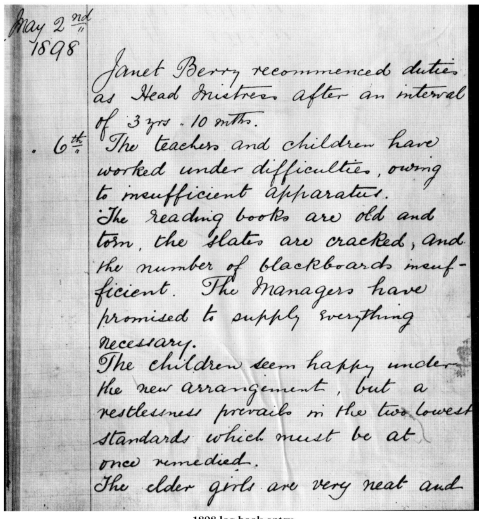

1898 log book entry
This records when Janet Berry recommenced duties as headteacher of the girls' school

Records indicate that during these eight years the two headteachers created two successful and highly regarded schools. Numbers increased steadily and there was now a total of over 400 pupils on the schools' books. Many of these did, though, attend school on a part-time basis, spending either the morning or afternoon working in local mills and quarries. Some Lightcliffe pupils spent their working hours at Brear and Brown's brewery in Hipperholme. We know that on one occasion it was recorded that 'mill boys in the afternoon did their dictation better than those in the morning'.

Away from the day-to-day matters regarding the pupils' education the schools' finances clearly exercised the managers' minds and were, for a period in 1881, overdrawn by almost £97. School fees continued and these were added to annually by a list of subscribers. There was the remarkable amount of over £33 raised in 1871 when the Bishop of Ripon, the then Diocesan Bishop as Wakefield Diocese was not formed until 1888, preached. This amounted to approximately three-quarters of the mistress's salary. At the time this was a common way of raising money for voluntary schools.

There was income too from the many outside groups that hired the school and the field. In March 1888 local farmer Christopher Holgate rented the field for, more than likely, sheep grazing. It was very much a 'community centre' as the founder hoped. Groups using the school included 'Gentlemen of the Neighbourhood' who in 1873 provided 'literary and musical entertainment in capital style' and the Band of Hope who provided equally popular entertainment. 1885 saw the first annual tea and entertainment of the Hipperholme and Lightcliffe football team take place in the school. In 1889 the cricket club paid 10s 6d and the Church Society £3 3s to use the premises. In the same year the Britannia Minstrels gave a concert and on a Saturday in May the annual meeting of the Halifax and District Teachers' Association was held in the school. The day included a visit to Crow Nest as guests of Sir Titus Salt and, on return, a 'sumptuous tea was heartily enjoyed'.

The school was also used by both the Sunday School and the Church Lads' Brigade on a more regular basis and usually without any problems. However, the following logbook entries indicate that this was not always the case:

Girls' School 19 January 1900

Much damage done to furniture and apparatus has been done to the day school lately by boys of the Sunday school. Offenders have been brought before the headmaster and vicar and threatened with the law.

Boys' School 29 January 1903

Managers held their monthly meeting. Their attention was drawn to the way in which boys of the Church Lads' Brigade had abused the privilege granted to them of using the school on the occasion of their pie supper. It was found that they had deliberately splashed the walls with ink and indulged in other forms of barbaric behaviour.

There are also interesting entries in the cash books for payments as this random selection shows: In 1872 a certain 'Higgins' [Thomas *Higgson* of Hipperholme] is recorded as earning 5s 6d for sweeping the chimneys; In 1888 James Sykes looked after the grounds for £2 2s 6d a quarter; Mr Dawson, a mason, was paid twelve shillings and a blacksmith, Mr Ellis, nine shillings. Mrs Lockwood cleaned the school for £3 18s a quarter and Mr Crossley received £154 for flagging the yard. Water closets were not installed until 1905 and for the unpleasant task of removing the 'nightsoil' (the contents were always removed at night) one J Wood was paid twelve shillings in December 1888, and David Smith was paid 19s 6d a quarter for cleaning them. A report of June 1900 indicates, however, that not all was well with the privies when school inspector S R Wilson had this to say:

I visited the school without notice and found that the latrines need the immediate attention of the managers.

Even after the installation of water closets, in 1905, the district sub-committee of the WRCC were 'shocked to find only one lavatory bowl for over 200 children' in the girls' school.

Finally before we move on to 1906, when the schools were once again amalgamated, a few extracts from the earliest logbooks to hand may not be out of place.

20 July 1894
The attendance throughout the week has been very poor. Gardeners' children are gathering fruit and farmers' children are haymaking.

22 June 1898
School closed for the afternoon. Halifax Fair.

22 July 1899
The gentlemen of Lightcliffe Golf Club have, during the last weeks, induced the boys not holding labour certificates to caddy for them. They wilfully break the law notwithstanding my repeated messages to them to that effect. They consider my calling their attention to this matter interfering.

2 October 1899
School opened. Headmistress not at school owing to storm-could not cross from the Isle of Man. Miss Clayton took management.

4 April 1900
Dr Marsden gave an address to the boys on the evil effects of smoking.

12 June 1901
The vicar, the Reverend JR Hill, came in today to say 'good bye'. He is going to Canada for six months' rest, being in very bad health just now. He promised to write to the upper standards descriptive letters of Canada, since Canada is part of the work of the current year.

2 June 1902
The news that peace was proclaimed (Boer War) was honoured by a half day's holiday.

2 January 1904
During the week special attention has been given to the boots. Boys grow careless about their boots when the field and the lanes are dirty.

1 September 1904
A service is being held in church during the time that the remains of the late vicar, Reverend JR Hill are being interred in Dumfriesshire ... No less than 55 boys are absent with their parents' consent in order to attend the service. He was much beloved by the children.

17 November 1905
Slates are quite abandoned in standards V, VI and VII and are used very seldom in standards I-IV.

Chapter Four

One School: 1906-1924

The two schools were again amalgamated and opened as a single unit on 2 April 1906. George Hague who as readers will recall, had been appointed head of the boys' School in 1898, was appointed head of the mixed school. This meant, of course, that Janet Berry again had to relinquish her position as headteacher. Her departure said the *Brighouse Echo* was a 'matter of regret'. After a time as a WRCC peripatetic teacher she became head of Bentley Road School in Doncaster. Janet Berry died in Hove on 15 April 1949 aged 84 years and is buried in Lightcliffe Churchyard.

There was now a total of 299 pupils on roll, all in mixed (boys and girls) classes with the exception of Standards V and VI as mixed classes were not, reported the *Brighouse News*, 'advisable'. George Hague clearly brought a very good reputation as head of the boys' school with him to support his added responsibilities. In 1902 the managers had received a report indicating that the school was conducted with 'skill and energy'.

Ethel Womersley recalled, again in 1969, George Hague's progressive innovations and how teachers from other schools, and inspectors came to observe his methods: his teaching of 'rapid addition' in arithmetic, his introduction of playlets and dramatic sketches, games teaching and country dancing. There was a large map of the world painted on the floor which fired the children's imagination with pictures of distant lands. Lantern slides were shown, enhancing the teaching of many subjects. It was the art work, though, that George Hague encouraged that drew most of the visitors and in 1908 the work was displayed at local exhibitions and at the North of England Conference in Bradford. There was praise from an inspector in 1910 who noted that, in addition to the school being well managed, there was 'much excellent work done in drawing and especially brushwork'. Other areas of the curriculum were not neglected and we read that in 1922 religious education was imparted with exceptional thoroughness and the 'fine singing' was an inspiration.

It is clear that the headteacher was a progressive educationalist but he also comes across as a kind and understanding personality. During the First World War a good number of evacuee children from the Channel Islands and Belgium attended the school, a pattern that was repeated some 30 years later, and both he and his wife made special provision for them and took them into their home to teach them the language. There was sadness, too, when one of them died shortly after leaving school and again when the airman brother of Miss Pohlman, a teacher, recorded as having been shot down, and that 'his machine had fallen in flames in German territory'.

George Hague with a class group in 1924

Much information about George Hague was collected in 1969 when former pupils came forward with invaluable schoolday memories that could so easily have been consigned to history. There were recollections of his way of dealing with boys who had been fighting. Mr J Varley remembered 'Daddy' Hague's way of sorting a problem with him and another boy who had been fighting'. He got us together and made us shake hands. Out of his pocket he produced two pennies, gave us one each, and told us to go down to Brown's shop for some sweets. I don't think that we ever thought of fighting each other again'. Mary Edley (née Goodger) who kept in touch with George Hague right up to his death at the age of 83, also recalled his method of dealing with those who became chalking pedagogues in their leisure time. Buckets and scrubbing brushes were supplied and every mark removed from the playground walls. There were recollections too of hot summer days when Mr Hague permitted teacher and children to leave their stuffy classrooms, in order to hear a story at the front of school under the weeping ash tree that was still to be seen well into the current century.

Although the reflection of these happy days is clear and affectionate the punishment book of the time gives us another side of school life. George Hague, as we have heard, knew when not to use the cane and he even recorded in 1908 the 'case was not definite for corporal punishment'. However, evidence before us shows that on a number of occasions, as was the order of the day, this was not the case! From 1908 he was, though, guided by a circular issued by the WRCC Education Committee which stated that:

Corporal punishment should in no case be inflicted, except for very grave offences, until other methods have been tried and have failed.

What were the offences that warranted the cane and what of the stories behind the punishments? We learnt much in 1969 from Wilfred Bottomley, a former pupil during the time of George Hague, and a number of his recollections are also recorded in the punishment book of the time. He recalled how many of the boys gleefully deceived the teacher who had sent them to the (head)master to be caned by blowing and rubbing their hands when they had never crossed the threshold of the masters room. We now know from the punishment book that the wheeze was eventually spotted and four boys were caned three times on each hand, and a girl twice. It was unusual for girls to be caned and records of such include few girls' names. However, we do know that initially the mistress of the girls' school possessed a punishment strap which was embossed 'Lightcliffe National Church school-Girls 1866'. This was still in the school in 1942 when it was used, recalled Leslie Morgan, on him.

A few 'classic' entries from the punishment book will, I think, be of interest, and in some cases, amusement to the reader—especially some of the pleas by the 'victims' and the master's additional comments.

1903 JN *Kicking small boy and sending impertinent message to headteacher.* Two strokes on hand

1903 LR, JN, HN, FH, FN, WD, GB. *Stealing apples from MR Hill's garden, Perth Villas.* Three with cane on hand and LR placed across chair.

1905 JN *Wilfully placed stick down privy and daubed the handles of the door.* Six strokes on each hand. Punishment witnessed by the vicar.

1905 JN *When told to write out five errors from dictation ran out to play.* Two strokes.

1905 JM *Making water on the field.* Two strokes on each hand.

1909 AF, RF, FG, HJ, GT. *Making a noise in the porch and calling out offensive names to Miss Roper.* Three strokes on each hand. FG also put across the desk.

1910 EC *When requested to alter a word in composition said 'I won't'. When caned said 'somebody will pay for this' and other impudent remarks.* Two strokes on each hand and then two more strokes.

1912 HN *Impertinence to teacher, Miss Womersley, after sweets confiscated. Threatened to bring father and said teacher would have to pay for them.* Three strokes on each hand.

It is interesting to note on looking through the book how often the same names (only initials shown here) appear over and over again. JN clearly was something of a serial offender!

All the punishments recorded were accompanied by the headteacher's 'remarks'. The following random entries are from the period 1903-12.

Boy called out to headteacher, 'Doctor says I haven't to be caned on my left hand. Doctor says so and I'm barn to tell him'.

Boy has grown beyond control of his parents and richly merited his punishment

Punishment merited in the best interest of the class. Other methods have little effect and are seen by the lads as weakness.

A bad lad. He has recently stolen from his parents a considerable amount of money.

This is the third case of the kind (apple stealing). R and B have previously been birched in Halifax for stealing a pigeon.

Corporal punishment had always been a contentious issue and there is clear evidence of mixed views on the matter. Some twelve years before the guidelines already referred to, there had been a lone campaign by the Lightcliffe Congregational Church Minister, the Reverend JH Stowell, who was concerned about the alleged excessive use of such in the school.

In a long letter published in the *Halifax Courier* in March 1896, and one to the Education Department, both retained in the National Archives, he expressed a number of concerns. Stowell's letter to the paper is clearly based on second-hand evidence but is of an accusatory nature. His main concerns centred around what he termed the 'brutality' of the discipline and the caning for trivial offences. The letter is long and hard-hitting and he concludes by charging the managers with having taken too little interest in the school discipline. In a further letter, to the Education Department, dated 10 March 1896 he writes:

In pursuing my duty here during the past three years I have come much into contact with the parents of children attending Lightcliffe National School and in consequence of their almost invariable dissatisfaction with the school. [There is no other evidence to this effect] I have of late taken some pains to investigate matters and I regret to say have, in many cases, found complaints well founded.

A member of staff throughout this period, and for much longer, was Miss Ethel Womersley. Hers is a remarkable story. She was born in December 1882, entered school in August 1887 and at the age thirteen became a pupil-teacher. At the time she was living at the White Horse Inn with other members of the family: Her father Crossley, mother Rose Ellen and siblings Gertrude 20, Vernon 19, Ella 16, Fred 14, Lily 12, Herbert 10, Ethel 8, Lucy 6, Jane 4 and Annie 2. Lily also became a teacher. She worked initially at the school as a pupil-teacher prior to transferring to Hipperholme Infants' School in 1894. She returned in 1918 as Mrs Hey and taught at the school until 1929.

Ethel Womersley returned to the school in July 1902 after being appointed as 'ex P.T. at a salary of £45 per annum'. Life was not easy for the young teacher during her early years as the following logbook extracts indicate:

1 August 1902
Standards one and two are in a very backward state. The teacher, Miss Ethel Womersley, has only had charge of the class for a fortnight and is therefore in no way responsible for this backwardness.

12 April 1906
Miss E. Womersley had to take charge of standard III and standard IV nearly 100 children—a very arduous task.

28 June 1907
Miss Womersley quite collapsed this morning at school. She has been suffering for nearly three years with her throat.

2 July 1907
Miss Womersley was at school this morning and remained for the day though quite unfit to be present.

Ethel Womersley remained at the school until she retired in 1947 after 45 years. She was then, and indeed remains, the longest serving teacher in the school's history. Her career embraces not just many chapters of this book but many generations of pupils. One such pupil was Ella Barnard who, as Ella Hirst, was able, in 1997, to give us a flavour of what life was like in Miss Womersley's classroom during the early part of the twentieth century. Ella attended school from 1905 and soon learnt that her teacher was the sister of her Godmother! She recalled that Ethel was quite a firm teacher and when Ella joined the golf club, where her former teacher was also a member, she found that Ethel 'hit the golf ball as hard as she used the cane'!

The caretaker during the period of Ella Barnard's school day was Francis Bradley who also acted as verger at St Matthew's Church. He is remembered as a meticulous caretaker. When he left in 1913, to become verger at St Hilda's Church in Halifax, George Hague recorded that it was 'with great regret that the managers lose his services'. It was Fanny his wife, though, who the pupils were especially going to miss as she made

Caretaker Francis Bradley and his wife.
(David Ellis collection)

outstanding rice puddings that were 'never to be forgotten'. They were made ostensibly for those who lived too far away from the school to go home for dinner but many others, including young Ella Barnard, joined the queue and willingly paid their penny. Francis and his wife later returned to Lightcliffe and records show them living in Till Carr Cottage in 1939, with Francis working as verger and sexton. He died in 1958, aged 83, and is buried in the churchyard he tended, along with his wife and their only child, Samuel, who died in infancy.

Many former pupils also remembered another caretaker, Benjamin Cross, long after they left the school. He was appointed in 1915 and worked at the school for 27 years. As in the case of Mrs Bradley, he is also remembered for the way, during his early days, he fed hungry mouths at lunchtime. He supplied slices of bread and dripping, spiced with a little salt and pepper, again for one penny.

Reminiscences afford a more intimate and personal picture of school during the early years of the twentieth century than do official records. However, extracts from the log books of the period do present a further picture of life at the school during George Hague's headship.

1 December 1906
Much good work has resulted throughout the school in arithmetic by classification according to ability.

12 December 1906
Muriel Burton, Standard II, was travelling by train from Hipperholme to Lightclffe this morning with her sister, Edna. On reaching the station they could not open the door and the train moved off. Muriel became excited and jumped out after the train had travelled several hundred yards ... fortunately she fell against a heap of soil and so only received a bruised and swollen head. Edna remained in the carriage until she reached Wyke.

24 January 1907
The classrooms (small rooms at each end of the school) have been so cold today that it has not been possible to use them. Temperatures of 34 and 37 taken at different periods,

13 March 1907
Several cases of petty theft. Children complain of missing their lunch oranges. Teachers have missed money that has been taken from their pockets.

26 November 1907
Managers complain that they have had to receive ten shillings less for rent for the grazing of the field, owing to boys making bare patches by their games and pastimes.

6 August 1913
Local cricket match between the police and a team of gentlemen was the cause of poor attendance in the afternoon.

11 November 1914
Belgian children (war evacuees) admitted.

24 May 1917
Two boys entered Lee's coal merchants and stole a penny which they spent at Mr Sutcliffe's sweet shop and then stole two packets of cigarettes.

One day towards the end of 1924 George Hague asked all the children to assemble in the school yard. He explained that he would retire shortly and before he did he would like the children to be photographed with him. Mrs Kathleen Briggs had, some twenty years ago, vivid memories of that occasion and recalled the sad expressions on every child's face as they heard the unheralded announcement.

An inspector's report around that time also shows the high esteem in which George Hague was held by those in higher authority:

The headmaster is reaching the close of a distinguished career at this school. His teaching has been chiefly characterised by a vivid style of address, which rivets the attention of the children. To the latter he allows a large measure of liberty but the strength of his personality prevents this from degenerating into license.

Chapter Five

The Headships of Herbert Marshall and John Ward: 1925-1944

The school reopened after the Christmas holidays on 5 January 1925. The children and staff were welcomed by the new headteacher, Herbert Clifford Marshall, who had joined the school after being head at Scissett CE School since 1908. He had previously taught at Dewsbury Road School in Leeds and at St Andrew's in Brighouse.

Overcrowding was one of the first issues facing the new headteacher as the health of the children in the small upstairs rooms was being affected. In one case 44 children were being accommodated in a space suitable for only 31. The County Council suggested that 33 children from the east of Stoney Lane should be transferred to Bailiff Bridge. The suggestion was not, however, taken up.

In 1926 a significant education report, the Hadow Report, was published under the title *The Education of the Adolescent.* This recommended the reorganisation of the nation's schools into primary to eleven years and secondary to fourteen, as the school leaving age then was, and preferably to fifteen to give a four-year course. It proposed a new type of school for the less academic— the modern senior school. It was a forerunner of the seminal 1944 Education Act. The West Riding County Council Education Department set to work on the ideas and formulated a wide-ranging set of proposals for the Brighouse and Hipperholme area. Lightcliffe, which at that time had around 84 seniors on roll, was to accommodate children of primary age only. Most of the suggestions failed to materialise until, as we shall hear, the 1944 Act.

Clearly Herbert Marshall continued the good work of his predecessor and, following a visit by His Majesty's Inspectors in 1930, it is recorded that the upward trend of the school was 'well maintained'. Arthur Haigh, a pupil

Herbert Marshall. Headteacher 1925-38

at the time, recalled in 1969 how the headteacher's love of literature encouraged pupils to read from the large collection of books that may have belonged to the church, stored in the old school house. The headteacher, remembered also as a 'perfect gentleman', may have still being living in the school house during his headship as Mr Haigh also recalled an amusing aside: Mrs Marshall apparently occasionally interrupted her husband's lessons when she appeared at the classroom door with curlers in her hair!

Another pupil at the time, Willie Tordoff, who lived at Glen Terrace, recalled how his mother handed him at the school wall a daily cup of egg, milk and sugar whisked together.

Senior boys (11-14 year olds) 1929

it was during Herbert Marshall's time as head that two old students' societies were formed. Lightcliffe Old Girls' Society began in 1935 and at its inaugural meeting chaired by the headteacher. Miss E Womersley was elected Secretary and Miss M Howells treasurer. Meetings and social functions were held regularly until 1941 but these then tailed off and the group was disbanded in April 1951. We also have evidence of an old boys' association. However, apart from a few events in school such as helping at sports' day and an annual dinner it appears to have met with little success.

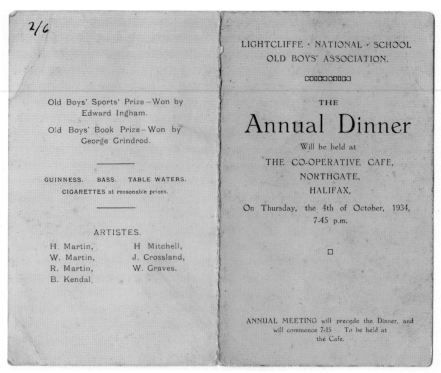

2/6

LIGHTCLIFFE · NATIONAL · SCHOOL
OLD BOYS' ASSOCIATION.

Old Boys' Sports' Prize—Won by
Edward Ingham.

Old Boys' Book Prize—Won by
George Grindrod.

GUINNESS.   BASS.   TABLE WATERS.
CIGARETTES at reasonable prices.

ARTISTES.

H. Martin,	H Mitchell,
W. Martin,	J. Crossland,
R. Martin,	W. Graves.
B. Kendal,	

THE

Annual Dinner

Will be held at

THE CO-OPERATIVE CAFE,
NORTHGATE,
HALIFAX,

On Thursday, the 4th of October, 1934,
7-45 p.m.

ANNUAL MEETING will precede the Dinner, and
will commence 7-15   To be held at
the Cafe.

Old Boys' Association annual dinner, 1934
(Courtesy of Leslie Morgan)

The following log book entries cover some of the more interesting comments made during Herbert Marshall's headship.

3 April 1925
Miss Kaye is to take charge of Hipperholme Infants' School in place of Miss Swift who is absent owing to the death of her mother.

23 September 1925
Emergency holiday this afternoon in order to prepare the school for a social event in connection with the Golden Jubilee celebrations at Lightcliffe Church.

29 June 1925
Today the installation of electric lighting in the school has been completed.

8 June 1926
Dr Brown visited school in connection with the WRCC arrangements about health week.

29 June 1927
School opened at 10am and closed at 12.35pm. This was in order that teachers who wished to visit the area of total eclipse of the sun might do so.

17 October 1927
During the week's closure the gallery has been removed from the middle room. Work in connection with the enlargement of the classroom [into what had originally been the master's house] at the west end of the school is still in progress.

9 May 1930
School played St Andrew's School in the final of the Turnwright Cup competition at Carr Green. Lightcliffe won, the score being 4 goals to 3.

19 January 1931
In connection with the issue of milk to the children, twelve children have been certified as being in such a condition that extra nourishment is necessary. Of those eight are to have the milk free of charge.

23 January 1934
The annual sports were held on the field on Saturday. All the staff were present together with several members of the Old Boys' Association. The latter gave valuable help in acting as stewards etc.

9 November 1934
Holiday for one day in honour of the marriage of HRH the Duke of Kent and Princess Marina of Greece.

19 January 1935
110 children attended the clinic at Hipperholme for immunisation against diphtheria.

3 May 1935
In connection with the Silver Jubilee of King George V, a souvenir bank book with a credit of one shilling is being presented to each child in attendance at a school under the WRCC. These along with souvenir pens and pencils were presented by Councillor J Lawson one of the managers.

6 November 1935
School closed today on the occasion of the marriage of the Duke of Gloucester to Lady Alice Montagu-Douglas-Scott.

20 April 1937
Swimming classes (boys) began at Brighouse Baths today.

22 April 1937
Girls' swimming classes begin today.

5 April 1938
In connection with health week, 150 of the elder children visited the Ritz Cinema in Brighouse to view health films

6 May 1938
The school football team beat St Martin's in the final of the Turnwright Cup.

Turnwright Cup winners 1938
Back row from the left: R Norminton, Donald Firth, John Norman, Colin Eastwood, Harry Ford, Harold Taylor, Ernest Barrett, H C Marshall.
Front row from left: Jack White, Percy Goddard, Norman Riley, George Lomas, Ernest Goddard, Leslie Beecroft.

The last log book entry made by Herbert Marshall was on 22 July 1938 when he had been granted leave of absence to attend his son's wedding. When school reopened after the summer holidays on 1 September a Mrs A Hartley, a County Supply headteacher, was in charge of the school. The headteacher had not been in good health for some time and his resignation, tendered on health grounds, took effect from the end of the year. Appreciation of his services were recorded at both a Brighouse Council meeting and at the school. Herbert Marshall died on 9 February 1941, aged 59.

John Ward appointed headteacher

On 27 January 1939 the managers had met and appointed John Ward of Hebden Bridge as successor to Herbert Marshall. We read from the managers' minutes that they had received applications from 61 candidates and had chosen five for interview. The new headteacher commenced duties on 1 May and was supported initially by the following members of staff: Robert Norminton, Oswald James and the Misses Phyllis Aspinall, Kathleen Kaye, Mary Marsh, Phyllis Sternthwaite and Ethel Womersley.

With the threat of war in Europe looming one of John Ward's first tasks was to organise an air raid exercise. We read from the log book that the school was successfully evacuated in two minutes. These precautions were certainly not precipitate as the following grim entries in the log book from 1939 show:

3 September 1939
Sunday. Britain declared war on Germany.

4 September 1939
School closed for one week owing to the state of emergency being declared. Teachers to remain at their posts during the week and to be available for any clerical work required by the Town Clerk.

For the next few years air raid drill became part of the school curriculum. Two air-raid shelters were erected in the playground and three on the school field. Former pupils will recall those in the playground remained in place until the first phase of extensions in 1966 and the ones on the field are now buried under the banking by the school service drive and the top playground. Each child was equipped with a gas mask and each knew his or her place in the shelters which were illuminated with storm lanterns.

It wasn't often that the children were summoned to the shelters. On one occasion when they did occupy them the excitement was such that, after a couple of hours singing and other diversions, the staff failed to hear that the 'all-clear' had been sounded. Kathleen Murray who, many will recall, taught at the school for 27 years until 1966, ventured out to see what was happening. A passer-by informed her that the signal had been given two hours previously!

It wasn't long after war was declared that the school roll, which stood at around 275, increased to some 380. This began slowly with the spasmodic arrival of refugees from countries and islands at risk of or under German occupation. The school admission register of the time provides us with details of the refugees and of the evacuees from within England who began to arrive from 1942.

The first refugee to arrive is recorded as twelve-year-old Kurt Singer from Austria who was admitted to the school on 25 September 1939. He resided at 32 The Grove before leaving for the refugee hostel in Ipswich the following May. During 1940 the first of many refugees from the Channel Islands was admitted to the school, when thirteen year-old Lillian Frances Newsom arrived from Guernsey. She lived at 12 Valley Avenue and left school, at the then minimum leaving age of fourteen, in April 1941. Forty-two more refugees were admitted during the next few years with the final group of three, from the Channel Islands, joining the school in September 1944.

Who were those who followed Kurt Singer and Lillian Newsom and where did they come from? Records show that the vast majority came from Alderney and Guernsey, and many came as whole families unlike the evacuees when it was just the children who came. For example, the Duquemin family from Guernsey came in September 1940. Father Ubert was a wire worker and the pupils admitted were his son, also called Ubert and daughters Brenda and Margaret. The Simonets from Alderney (John, Alfred and David) were admitted to the school in the October. In November of the same year three members of the Gallichan family (Mona, Ruth and Kenneth) aged 12, ten and seven respectively were admitted. Two more siblings, William, 13 and

George, aged five, joined them five weeks later in January 1941. It appears that the family returned to Guernsey in 1947. Most, although not all, of the other refugees also returned home once the Channel Islands were liberated.

We wrote in 1997 that Barbara Garnier, who joined the school in 1941 from Alderney, as her siblings Sonia and Gladys did at a later date, remained here and subsequently married Walter Scott who was closely involved with what became the Lightcliffe United Reformed Church (now Christ Church). In 1941 the family resided at 15 Hill Top in Lightcliffe and were later joined by what appear to be cousins, Fay, Peter and Michael. It looks from the records as though their fathers were brothers who both worked as labourers at Brooke's quarries and brickworks.

Members of the family of Walter Barrand from Alderney also remained here and it is good to report that Brian Barrand is still living in the area. It is through Brian and his wife Patricia (née Healey), that I have been able to form a more detailed picture of the refugees who came from the Channel Islands. The eldest member of the family, David, was admitted to the school in September 1941 and his siblings followed during the next five years, Brian in 1943. As they lived at Fenay House, all attended Hipperholme Infants' school initially. Their father, Walter, also worked at Brooke's and both Brian and his wife wonder if the connection with the company's quarries in the Channel Islands was the link with the work that so many of the men found in the area. There were other members of the family here also: children of Brian's father's sisters, Daniel Acquetil, Beryl and George Chapman had been admitted form Alderney in August 1940 and resided at 16 Brookeville, Hipperholme.

The first evacuees, overwhelmingly from the south east and Hull, began to arrive in late 1940. There is little hard evidence initially in the admission register, initially, as to who is an evacuee. The 'withdrawal' column along with the destination and the length of stay, was initially, our only clue as to who was an evacuee.

From 1942, however, when the system became more organised there is clear evidence to indicate which pupils were admitted as evacuees. Between June and August 1944, 135 children were admitted as such and more were to follow. A little information in relation to these children—where they came from, where they lived, how long they stayed may not be out of place at his stage.

The first evacuee to be admitted, on 16 September 1940, *appears* to be Barbara Pryor from Barking who returned home after just a few months. Jean Lyons from Hull, Daphne and Colin Andrews from Colchester, Jill and Peter Farrar from Sevenoaks, Ruth Coe from Streatham and Veronica and Michael from Twickenham followed shortly afterwards. These all returned home in 1941.

It was, as indicated, from Hull (51 evacuees) and the south-east, especially the Medway towns of Strood (29), Rochester (17) and Chatham (13) that the majority of the children came. Other south-eastern towns including Ilford, Mottingham, Dagenham, Sidcup and Bexleyheath sent in total a further 70. On looking at a few of the children's names we do find many examples of three or four siblings arriving together. For example, Miriam, Arthur, Margaret and Phyllis Andrews from Hull whose father, Albert, a timber dock worker (most of the children from Hull had fathers who worked in the docks as fish porters, fishermen, and shipbuilders) who had been unemployed for four years, arrived in June 1942 and stayed at number 2 The Crescent. They returned home fifteen months later. The five Childs' children from Sidcup, along with their mother Violet, arrived in 1944 and resided at Holly Bank.

The four Nicholls children from Dagenham were accommodated at three separate addresses off St Giles Road with Mesdames Marshall, Cracknell and Smith. Three properties on The Grove (numbers 11,26 and 27) housed the three Diffey children from Strood who joined, respectively, the Daw, Culpan and Smith families. The four Everest children were housed in Priestley Green with the Goldthorp, Measham and Dowson families. The vicar Canon Taylor and his wife played their part also, and in 1944 they welcomed two children from Rochester and Strood to the vicarage.

On 4 September 1944 a group of 21 children listed as 'flying bomb evacuees' were admitted from Kent and Middlesex. Flying bombs, otherwise known as doodlebugs, were early cruise missiles and extremely unpredictable. Virtually all these children returned home within three months. The final evacuee to attend the school was David Curtis from Hull who was admitted as late as March 1945. He was back home in less than three months.

One story regarding the evacuees that is recorded in the log books concerns the Rochester headteacher, Louis Nobbs, who had accompanied the children to Lightcliffe. During October 1944 he had to return home for one week to identify belongings from his blitzed home. Mr Nobbs taught many of the evacuees in the temporary accommodation that was made available at the Bramley Lane schoolroom. Miss Margaret Rushworth, a colleague who had accompanied him, taught the infants in the main school.

In addition to the arrival of the large number of additional pupils there were other reminders of the war. At a meeting in October 1940 the managers were made aware of a letter from the Director of Education in relation to scrap metal for war purposes. They were asked if they would be willing to offer the iron railings on the boundary walls. The matter was put in abeyance in the hope that there would be sufficient metal elsewhere. However, as can be seen along Wakefield Road, most of the railings were later removed. Two years later the managers discussed insufficient staffing following the departure of the two teachers to the armed forces. They expressed the hope ' that married women be eligible for appointment for the duration of the war' which was not the case at the time. One class, it was reported, had had eight teachers in five months.

'Digging for victory' was also very much a feature of school life during this period. The *Brighouse Echo* reported in June 1940 that the scholars of Lightcliffe School had been 'doing their bit' for the national campaign. One third of an acre in the north-western corner of the school field was used as gardens and the indications were that a 'bumper crop' would result.

In amongst all this wartime activity it is recorded that a school meals service began at the school. Prior to this the children who lived some way from the school had brought sandwiches or, in some cases, had taken a midday meal at the 'British

Restaurant' that was situated on the top floor of the old Liberal Club at Hipperholme. Leslie Morgan remembered with great glee in 1969 that he was the first pupil to be served there! After the first meals were served in the school John Ward reported that the service and the meals were 'very satisfactory'. One of those serving the meals was Mrs M Hartley who, at the time of the school's centenary, was still serving meals at the school. The managers did, however, continue to discuss the desirability of a kitchen being built at the school in place of a scullery. This they said, in 1946, would save money on the delivery of containers and improve the nutritional value of the food. (Their wish was finally granted in 1984!)

It was during John Ward's headship that perhaps the key education bill of the century was introduced into parliament by education minister Richard Austen Butler. This bill, which became law in August 1944 marked a new era in educational thinking. Following this Act children were to be educated according to ability and aptitude and not simply according to age. Education was to be divided into three parts: primary, secondary and further. Three types of secondary schools were to be created: grammar, secondary modern and technical, with the leaving age raised to 15. This is not the place to discuss the success or otherwise of these proposals, but the restructuring of the system and other sections of the act were to have an effect on this school.

Perhaps the most noticeable result was the change in the age groups that the school accommodated. By the September children over the age of eleven proceeded to other schools, chiefly St Martin's in Brighouse. The school would now cater for infants and juniors only.

Dedication of the flagpole 1943, with John Ward and Canon Harold Taylor

The Act also had an effect on some 'second-tier' education authorities. A number of the smaller ones, such as Brighouse, were subsumed into larger ones and became part of County Education Authorities. The school was to become part of the Ashlar Division of the West Riding Education Committee with its offices at the now demolished Manor House in Brighouse.

An end-of-term concert marked the end of an era for the school. There were songs, plays and dances performed by each class. Form prizes were awarded as follows: first prizes to Sonia Barrett, Kathleen Berry, Ann Ellis, Bernard Jaques, Marie Noble, Phyllis Platt, Pauline Simpson, June Taylor and Margaret Walker. Second prizes went to Jean Denton, Irene Jackson, Marian Jones, June Low, David Maude, Dennis Norton, Kenneth Padgett, Margaret Sanderson, Peter Sladdin and Graham Wood. A special gardening prize, in relation to the 'Dig for Victory' effort was awarded to Royston Hutchinson. He received National Savings Certificates given by Councillor Milton Barritt. The *Brighouse Echo* noted that following reorganisation, Miss Olga Ashworth was transferring to Brookfoot School. Scholars and staff had presented her with an 'electric reading lamp' at the same event.

Log book entries from the beginning of the war to the 1944 Education Act include:

25 October 1939
Headmaster arrived at 10.15am after being on duty all night at the telephone exchange as a special constable.

19 April 1940
The collection of eggs for local hospitals in response to an appeal made by the Mayoress of Brighouse resulted in a total of 1,542.

27 June 1940
Through overcrowding of the 1.20pm bus, boys attending woodwork classes at St Martin's Centre were 15 minutes late.

12 July 1940
After receiving several complaints re the alleged use of the slipper by Mr ... as a means of corporal punishment, he was given permission to use slight corporal punishment provided he used the cane.

16 July 1942
Benjamin Cross, who commenced duties as caretaker of the school on 1 April 1915, died suddenly this morning after serving faithfully and efficiently for over 27 years.

16 July 1942
The wall separating the boys' and girls' playgrounds was taken down on the instructions of the managers.

7 July 1943
During the night a gale force wind blew the weather cock from the top of the school building into the garden. The weather cock was smashed.

24 May 1943
Empire day. A flag and staff placed in the school grounds by Miss Maud Hayles in memory of her niece Ethel Hayes, an old scholar, was this morning dedicated by Canon HL Taylor, MA.

Digging for Victory c1940

1 October 1943
Souvenir savings books, each bearing one shilling in stamps presented to each child by the Mayor of Brighouse to commemorate the Jubilee of the Incorporation of the Borough of Brighouse. (1893-1943).

13 October 1943
The lock of a cupboard in the hall was found open this morning. The youth movement met in this room last night.

23 January 1944
Youth movement meeting in school last night. Rude writing discovered on blackboard in the infant room.

25 July 1944
Headmaster visited the Department of Education relative to making arrangements for keeping the school open during the summer holidays for evacuated children.

18 January 1945
Youth club met in school last night. Damage was done viz:
a) Two school gramophone records were broken and pushed behind pipes.
b) Considerable chalking on tops and inside desks, and deliberate cutting with knife of PT apparatus box.
c) Push-pull switch of radiogram out of order.
d) Dining tables and kitchen draining board left in filthy condition.

Chapter Six

Lightcliffe Church of England Primary School

After the summer holidays, on 4 September 1944, the school reopened as a Primary (Junior and Infant) School with 368 children on roll. With the exception of a small number of older evacuee children all the senior pupils had transferred to St Martin's Secondary School in Brighouse. The school was still officially known as Lightcliffe National School. The change of name took place in early 1949 when the managers agreed, on 28 January, to a request from the Divisional Education Officer, that the school should now to be known as Lightcliffe CE Primary School.

Shortly after the change of name there was a change of caretaker when Mary Cross retired. Mrs Cross had fulfilled the role following the death of her husband in, as indicated above, 1942. She was presented with a sum of £10 1s as a token of 'affection and appreciation', following a collection. She was replaced by her son-in-law William Joseph Berryman, who would have been pleased to hear that the managers had agreed to install electricity in the school house. The work cost £20. The downside to the good news was that the managers then raised the rent to £11 per annum!

Ethel Womersley's retirement followed shortly after the caretaker's, on 19 December 1947. Her career began, as we have heard, on 1 July 1902. Throughout the school's history many teachers have taught at the school for long periods and their names are recorded here in the appendix. However, Miss Womersley's 45 years' service to the school is not only, as previously indicated, the longest but must be high on a national list of long service to one school.

On the day before her retirement she was presented with a silver salver by the Vicar, Canon Harold Lancaster Taylor, on behalf of the managers, staff and scholars. John Ward, the headteacher, spoke warmly of her loyalty, strong sense of duty and her untiring energy in the work of the school. Long after her retirement following 'many very happy years', pupils still recalled her other attributes: her phenomenal memory, general knowledge, musical ability and her sunburnt hands skilfully tending plants in the school garden.

The following year, 1948, saw another major retirement from the school: that of John Ward on 30 July after 'a very happy nine years at the school'. He was to take up the headship of Claremont Primary School in Blackpool. On the day prior to his departure he was presented with a wireless set, extension speaker and a cheque in the presence of the whole school, parents, friends and staff. His departure, indicated the *Brighouse and Elland Echo* was 'greatly regretted' and he had during his stay at Lightcliffe 'greatly endeared himself to hundreds of people by his genial and approachable personality'. The paper had already referred to him in glowing terms some five years earlier when he was elected president of the Brighouse Head Teachers' Association. He had, we read, 'long been known as a progressive and active spirit in the educational world'.

John Ward is remembered also as a popular headteacher in Blackpool. His time there was recalled, in 1997, by a former member of staff, Peggy Lynas, who described him as a fine head with a most encouraging sense of humour. She also recalled school visits from Blackpool to York and how eager Mr. Ward was to point out Lightcliffe School as the train either stopped at, or steamed through, the local station. How sad all his former colleagues were to learn of his death at the age of 67, only four years after retirement.

George Armitage appointed headteacher

George Armitage took up his appointment as headteacher on 1 November 1948 following his appointment on 23 July. He had previously been the head of St Michael's Boys' School in Wakefield. He was to lead a team of seven teachers: Mrs E Smart, J Crossley, RN Lister, Miss PM Aspinall and Mrs K Murray, who taught the junior classes, and Miss M. Hemingway (later headteacher of Hipperholme Infants' School) and Mrs E Edwards the infant classes. There were 295 pupils on roll and the class sizes, not untypical at the time, were: 40,40,41,42 and 43 in the juniors and 46 and 43 in the infants.

The headteacher introduced a number of innovations during the early years of his time in charge. Typical of these was the school's first Open Day on 14 June 1950. During the afternoon a large number of parents visited the classrooms and, we read from the logbook entry, took a 'genuine interest in the children's work'. A film show followed along with tea and biscuits and a bring and buy sale. The event is recorded as being 'a great success'.

Sports' day had been a regular summer function for many years but in 1950 children were no longer running for red, yellow, blue and green teams but for a newly introduced house teams named after the well-known local families of Ripley, Firth, Walker and Foster.

A few years later a school uniform, that survives to this day, was introduced. It is, however, clear from photographs that this was not initially worn by all the pupils or, indeed, during the decades that followed. This consisted of dark green blazers, gabardines, caps or berets and yellow and green striped ties. George Armitage and his staff designed an impressive badge to be worn on the blazers and headwear. This badge, which depicts the Bible, Yorkshire Rose, Prince of Wales Feathers and a cross, is still used today on clothing and stationery.

Many annual full-day educational visits for junior pupils were organised from shortly after George Armitage's arrival at the school. Former pupils will recall assembling on the platform at Lightcliffe Station and awaiting special trains to such places as

Newcastle (1952 and 1955), Chester (1953 and 1961)), Liverpool and New Brighton (1954 and 1959), Newcastle (1955), York(1956), Bowness (1957), London (1958) and Tyneside (1960). The itinerary of the 1954 visit to Liverpool is still to hand. The train left Lightcliffe at 9.28am and the other key times were as follows:

11.20am   Arrive Liverpool Exchange Station
11.50am   Conducted tour of docks and overhead railway
12.50pm   Tour of city and visit to cathedral
2.00pm   Via Mersey tunnel to New Brighton
3.00pm   Take lunch at Tick Tock Cafe and time on the beach
5.30pm   Cross the Mersey on ferry boat
8.41pm   Arrive Lightcliffe.

The three key events during George Armitage's headship were the question of aided status for the school, the first extensions to the foundation building, and the opening of a second primary school in Lightcliffe, namely Cliffe Hill.

The move towards aided status was the direct result of section 15 of the 1944 Education Act. The 'Dual Contract' of schools was seen by HL Dent as one of the outstanding triumphs of the act which named three categories of voluntary school: aided, controlled and special agreement. There would be more expense if aided status was chosen but there were advantages to be considered. The managers clearly had an important decision to make regarding the future of the school and they decided in December 1952 to seek aided status. .

During the following year Canon HL Taylor, the chairman of the managers, wrote to local people asking for their support and spelling out the advantages of voluntary aided status. Such status meant that the foundation managers would remain in a majority of four (including the principal officiating minister) to two representative managers (one elected by the LEA, the other by Brighouse Council), staff selection would remain in their hands, religious education would be in accordance with the trust deed and the managers would continue to 'own' the building, along with 'other benefits'. They would be responsible for the upkeep of the external fabric but would receive a grant for the work. The internal repairs and decorating would be the responsibility of the local authority. Aided status was granted on 13 November 1953. Around the same time the Lightcliffe managers relinquished full control of Hipperholme Infants' School. They had been responsible for the infants' school since April 1897 after the trustees agreed to place it under the jurisdiction of the Lightcliffe Management Board. The school then became voluntary controlled in 1954.

Following the decision to continue to accept responsibility for the buildings the managers needed further support. Following a meeting of the Parochial Church Council a Building Fund Committee was formed in February1953. Present on that winter's evening in addition to the vicar and the curate (GS Gilby), were Messrs Armitage, Barritt, Johnson, Leather, Ramsden, Mrs Robinson and Miss Dixon. They were to form the nucleus of the committee to be established to assist in 'raising money to attain aided status for the school' and to encourage others to support them. The additional group included Mesdames Knowles of Stoney Lane, Richardson of Cliffe Avenue, Briggs of Knowle Top Drive, Turner of Stoney Lane, Greenhalgh of

Boys' Athletics Team, 1951 with GL Armitage (left) and B Wildsmith

Class group 1956

Class group 1957

Class group 1958
The writer of the book's *foreword* is pictured in the centre of the back row.

Class group 1959

Class group 1959

Sutherland Road, Brear of Oak Mount, Poppleton of Sutherland Road and Mr E Brooke of Newton House. Many of these people served for many years well into the 1970s, as did others who joined later, such as Mrs Jean Bottomley from 1956.

The organisation was renamed the Development Association in 1984 with a wider brief and then, more recently, the Parents, Friends and Staff Association (PFSA). The fund-raising continues and the group now supports many initiatives introduced by the school by holding, for example, car boot sales, the long-standing Christmas Fair, 'Fun' evenings, and discos. The group's role in supporting the managers (later governors) ceased some time ago.

Thoughts of extending and upgrading the school were first discussed by the managers in 1946. They felt then that the suggested improvements as proposed by the West Riding Education Department's Development plan were inadequate especially as a local housing estate development of 334 properties was in the course of preparation. What they did not realise at the time, though, was that there were now firm plans for an additional school in the area. The proposed school, Cliffe Hill, referred to initially as Crow Nest School, was first mentioned at a managers' meeting in 1949. This new school at Stoney Lane opened on 1 September 1952 when 236 pupils were admitted. One member of the Lightcliffe staff, J Crossley, transferred to the new school along with some 30 children who lived on the new estate at addresses such as Fairless Avenue and Shirley Grove.

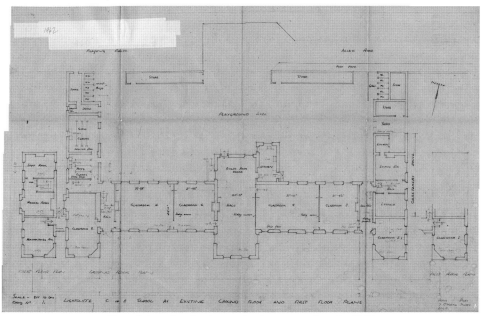

Plan of the school prior to the first extensions in 1966.
The lines indicating the sliding screens, that divided the large rooms what were once the boys' and girls' schools, can be seen along with the one that was folded back from the former infants' school in the centre to form a raised stage.

Clearly, though, there was still a need to improve the substandard and outdated facilities and the managers met in earnest at the vicarage in December 1962. It was then that they considered draft plans presented by Kenneth Jones of Messrs Jones and Stocks, Architects. Further meetings were held and eventually the plans, with some modifications, were accepted. One minor stumbling block was the boiler. The managers wanted an oil-fired boiler but the Authority's 'declared policy' was for solid fuel (coal).

Pickles of Halifax were appointed as builders and work began in April 1966. Clearly there was going to be a need to remove some of the children from the building owing to the cramped conditions that would prevail. This matter was addressed in two ways: by the hiring of a large prefabricated classroom that arrived one icy day just before the work commenced and by renting classroom space within the area. On 6 May two classes, along with teachers Harold Laycock and Geoffrey Hudson, were evacuated to rented accommodation at Hipperholme Methodist Church schoolroom. The agreement between the trustees and the County Council was for the daily letting of three rooms from 8.30 to 4.30pm, the hall and the kitchen for two and a quarter hours at lunchtime for the serving of meals, and the main hall also on Tuesday afternoons. Additional toilet provision was provided by a 'temporary structure'. The agreement also contained one somewhat bizarre clause making clear that the County Council:

Hereby undertake with the landlords not to allow betting or gambling in any form, nor the use of the premises for the sale or consumption of alcoholic beverages, nor for any other purposes contrary to the standing orders of the Methodist Conference.

Ashlar Sports Cricket Trophy winners 1964
From the left. Back: Philip Radcliffe, Roger Horner, Peter Kiernan, John Albutt, Richard Noble
Seated: Robert Sandie, Richard Spivey, Peter Pickard, Stephen Sandie, John Stead
Front: Michael Kershaw, Keith Guy

The additions and alterations to the foundation building included a new section running along the north face. This incorporated a corridor, cloakrooms and toilets, staff room, headteacher's room and a temporary kitchen. The internal alterations to the existing building included a new upstairs classroom at the western end, combining what were formerly the headteacher's, medical and staff rooms. Folding partitions between the rooms were replaced by solid walls although the one between the hall (once the infants' school) and the classroom to the east remained and was still, until the second phase of extensions, folded back for certain functions. The building now had a completely different feel to it and pupils and staff no longer had to walk through classrooms to move from one end of the building to the other.

On 26 May 1967 the two classes which had been housed at Hipperholme returned. George Armitage recorded that 'we now have all the classes under the same roof but the building work is far from finished'. The builders finally left in September of that year and phase one of the planned development programme was completed. The cost of these commodious extensions was £26,000.

It was during the period of George Armitage's headship that the Ashlar Schools' Sports' Association was formed and the first sports meeting was held on 21 June 1951. Fifteen Lightcliffe pupils competed in races with other schools in the area and three classes went along as spectators. The headteacher recorded with pride that 'the boys' and girls' trophies were both won by this school and the children did very well indeed'. More success followed over the years at this annual event held at either Brighouse Cricket Field or Waterloo Road Playing Fields. During this period the school teams also excelled in football, cricket, netball and rounders, as they had even before the First World War.

Recorder group 1965
Pictured with the author are from the left. *Back row:* Ruth Collins, Jane Palin, Deborah Thorpe, Charles Boylan, Michael Kershaw, Linda Walker, Margaret Horne, Christine Baines.
Front: Angela Naylor, Judith Raw, Barbara Catto, Elaine Collins, Jennifer Foyston, Lesley Hinchcliffe. Readers will note the grim outbuildings, that included staff and boys' toilets, that were demolished during the first phase of extensions.

After almost nineteen years as head of the school, George Armitage retired on 21 July 1967. During his last week at the school staff and pupils presented him with a dinner and tea service as a token of their thanks and respect. Deputy headteacher Harold Laycock, the chairman of the managers Canon F White, and staff member Marjorie Nuttall each spoke and mirrored those sentiments. The couple left Lightcliffe for Harrogate shortly afterwards and later moved to Hutton's Bosworth in Northamptonshire. It was there on Christmas Day 1991 that George Armitage died just one week after his wife, Elsie.

Below are some of the more interesting log book entries during the period covered by this chapter.

24 March 1945
To facilitate the delivery of milk and meals the gateway (Knowle Top Road) has been widened.

4 February 1947
Blizzard continued day and night. 146 children present.

17 July 1947
The caretaker reported that the Youth Group had been using the hall for alleged 'dirt track racing' on bicycles.

10 November 1947
Headmaster measured and weighed children for additional clothing coupons—59 qualified.

28 October 1948
Miss Kaye, who leaves the staff tomorrow after 40 years' service, was presented with a silver coffee jug by Canon Taylor on behalf of the managers and staff. [Another example of outstanding service to the school, the second longest in the school's history]

16 March 1949
A rat was again reported in the kitchen [This appears to have been an ongoing problem and was raised by the head at more than one managers' meetings]

29 March 1949
Another rat was seen in the kitchen at dinner time.

27 July 1949
After the holiday Miss Hemingway commences as headmistress of Hipperholme Infants' School.

2 May 1950
Today eight 40 Ibs boxes of apples arrived. These were a gift from the President of the British Columbia Tree Fruits Association and came through the Commonwealth Gift Centre. Each child received one pound of fine eating apples.

19 February 1954
All the junior classes were taken to the Ritz Cinema, Brighouse to see the film 'Conquest of Everest'.

30 September 1955
The vicar, Canon H L Taylor, died early this morning at the age of 77 and thus completed exactly 41 years as Vicar of this parish.

28 May 1956
Mrs Edwards was absent this afternoon to attend the mayor making ceremony at Brighouse where her husband became mayor and she became mayoress.

20 June 1956
The Divisional sports were held this afternoon. The girls again won the Girls' Cup; this has been the fifth time in six years.

27 June 1958
The list of children who have passed the selection for Grammar Schools arrived this afternoon. It contained 32 names.

21 February 1961
Today the new B.I.H. 16mm sound projector was used for the first time.

16 February 1962
The staff room ceiling fell in this morning due to the gale. At 1.30 part of the roof blew off and slates began to fall. The majority of the children were sent home in the interests of safety.

19 March 1966
The six-a-side football team won the knock-out competition cup at Waterloo Road.

The author's class in 1965.
Janis Timmons (see school report, p.52) is pictured seventh from the left on the front row.

School report 1964
Janis Carmichael (née Timmons) has kindly agreed to allow me to use her 1964 report that is so typical of those written at the time. Readers will no doubt smile at my comments under physical education.

Long division exercises, 1965
Calculations in miles, furlongs, chains and gallons, quarts, pints etc were still commonplace in 1965. These examples are selected from a nine-ten year old's book.

Harold Laycock's class 1965-66.
These pupils were shown as a younger group on p.51

Chapter Seven

A Period of Expansion

From the late 1960s until the end of the following decade the number of pupils on roll grew by some 40% as the so called 'bulge' passed through school. A report in the *Brighouse Echo* on 22 May 1970 entitled' Battle of the Bulge is being fought in schools' gave a clear picture of the situation in the Brighouse area. The problem was clearly not just Lightcliffe's but the figures at the school make compelling reading. The numbers had risen from 281 in 1960 to 336 and were expected to grow. We now know that by 1973 there were 400 pupils on roll and, by 1976, 440—an all time high. (They reached, as we shall hear, 437 in 1994, following the closure of two local schools.) Many of the extra pupils lived in the 1960s housing developments at Westfield Avenue, Westfield Drive and Park Close along with, for example, The Drive and Astral Avenue.

The rapid increase in numbers was a key issue that had to be addressed by the managers during the beginning of the headship of George Armitage's successor, Reginald Norman Lister, who had been appointed during the summer of 1967 and commenced duties in January 1968. Immediately prior to his appointment Mr Lister had been headteacher at St Augustine's School in Halifax and before that headteacher at St Chad's School at Hove Edge. He began his teaching career at Lightcliffe on 14 March 1949.

The fifteen-year period during which Norman Lister was headteacher at Lightcliffe will be remembered for many reasons: the rapidly increasing numbers as indicated, the accommodation problems and subsequent second-phase of extensions, the widening horizons with curriculum-linked day visits and residential visits, the many sacred and secular celebrations and the numerous local discussions centred around the reorganisation of schools in Brighouse.

It was but three months after he arrived that the managers met on 1 April and again on 6 May to discuss the phase-two extensions with the architect, Kenneth Jones. The discussion centred not just around further improvements but the issue of space to accommodate, as already indicated, the ever growing number of children seeking a place. Additional classrooms and a new hall were badly needed. The existing hall (the infants' school in the nineteenth century) was far too small. It was a great relief to the headteacher and the teaching staff when formal approval was granted for the planned extensions to go ahead in 1971. Short-term relief came in the form of more 'mobile' classroom provision. The contract for the extensions, which were to cost around £35,000, was awarded to Roberts of Leeds. The additional provision: the large hall, two adjacent classrooms, and a new scullery kitchen to replace the one that became a games and PE equipment store, was brought into use in February 1972. There were still, though, no facilities for meals to be cooked on the premises.

Building Fund Bring and Buy Sale 1968
In the happy group pictured are Mrs Rosalind Halliday (second left) and her mother, and then from third left, Mrs Ethel Pennington, Margaret Jackson, Katie Boylan and Mrs Shirley Dyson.
Fiona Dyson is at the front

Staff 1969
From left, back: Elaine Titley, Jennifer Brooke, Leslie Briggs, Margaret Hudson, Susan Cawkwell, Madge Laycock.
Front: Jeanne O'Rourke, Susan Dobson, Norman Lister, Marjorie Nuttall, Betty Carney.

Norman Lister recorded that the whole school used the new hall for the first time on 3 March 1973 and just one week later everyone gathered again, this time to say goodbye to the vicar, the Reverend Canon Frank White. Mr White had been vicar and chairman of the managers for almost seventeen years. The official opening and dedication of the extensions by the Right Reverend Eric Treacy took place on 23 June. There were many guests including George Armitage and his wife, present and former members of staff, parents and friends of the school. Norman Lister recorded that 'the school looked very attractive with flowers and displays. it was a very happy event with many old friendships renewed'.

This was not, as we shall hear, the end of the extensions. A library was added in 1977 thanks to the generosity of the Building Fund Committee and by the end of the decade the managers were meeting again to discuss further additions to the buildings. In June 1980 the Chairman of Governors (the term managers was now a thing of the past), the Reverend David Wilding wrote to the Chief Education Officer outlining some areas of concern: the two temporary mobile classrooms still in place, two very small classrooms at the eastern end of the school still in use, and inadequate staff toilet facilities and office accommodation.

In 1975 the problem of parking outside the school during the beginning and end of the school day was becoming a major problem and resulted in Norman Lister writing to the parents and asking for their help. 'I am extremely concerned', he wrote, 'about the hazard caused to children attending the school ... by parents who are dropping off or collecting their children.' He appreciated that the problem was 'compounded by cars belonging to the staff' and the need for a staff car park. This has continued to be a problem, despite the provision of a staff car park in 1990, as it has at many other schools. The associated dangers were even raised by HMI as 'a matter of great concern' in 1988.

It was around this time that the question of the future of Hipperholme Infants' School was also discussed by the governors. They were, however, unhappy that any extensions they were planning should be linked overtly with the closure of the Hipperholme School. The Lightcliffe governors did want to extend the school but not at the expense of the Hipperholme school in 'the way proposed by the education committee'. There was, as we shall hear, a different outcome to this situation ten years later.

Shortly after the LEA had agreed to keep the Hipperholme school open there was a different story at Norwood Green. The numbers at the school there were little more than 20 and it closed at the end of the 1983 summer term. The Norwood Green School had a long history. It was founded in 1819 and enlarged in 1882 at a cost of £220 which was raised by public subscription. In 1888 new trust deeds were executed which vested control in the hands of twelve trustees. A small housing development now occupies the site but the Ephraim Ellis memorial clock tower remains as a local landmark.

It was not, though, all about extensions and school closures during Norman Lister's headship. During his first summer at the school residential educational visits began. Mr Lister engendered a great love of the countryside and the initial visit, to Hebden near Grassington, was the first of many residential trips that continue to this day. This took place over a weekend during the summer of 1968 and he would have been encouraged by the support that he received from seven members of staff and, in a number of cases, their partners. The party stayed at 'Wharfedale Holidays', a wooden building close to the River Wharfe.

A sylvan scene at Rievaulx Abbey in 1968
8-9 year olds on a day's educational visit with teacher Jennifer Brooke.

He recorded in the school logbook that 'the fine weather enabled a full programme of work to be carried out during a most enjoyable weekend'. Former pupils in the party will recall the many fossil, wild flowers, birds and water creatures observed. They will remember also the eight-mile walk on the Saturday via Grassington and Linton, swimming in the Wharfe and the visit to Burnsall Church.

The centre at Hebden was used annually until 1974 when the pupils visited 'Hammarbank' in the Lake District and the following year Robin Cottage, also in the Lake District. The 1980s saw visits to Marrick Priory near Reeth and Newton House, near Whitby. Happily, the philosophy behind these educational and enjoyable visits instigated by Norman Lister still endures. One wonders, though, if his reminder to the children to 'always make sure that you have washed the pattern off your new bar of soap before returning home' has ever been carried out!

Hebden weekend 1968
A group on Linton packhorse bridge

Hebden weekend 1969
Pupils ready for the day ahead. Teacher Marjorie Nuttall can be seen third from the left
on the back row.

The 1970s will also be remembered for the many projects that involved the whole school. These were, for example, based around the work of the Church Missionary Society and involved many curriculum areas being drawn together for a 'Zaire' or 'Nepal' evening which usually included a 'local' dish. Finally, there was 'Hoppity' the friendly little gnome who, apparently, lived with the headteacher. His many imaginary adventures and journeys were often relayed, with a moral point, to the children during assemblies. One child, Norman Lister remembered, even called at the headteacher's house to ask if Hoppity was playing out!

As Norman Lister's retirement approached there was a staff party and later a 'This Is Your Life' evening when present and past colleagues, governors and many friends gathered and shared their reminiscences. There were gifts for the headteacher, including a splendid pottery model of the school . He in turn presented the school with items of furniture made by a Littlebeck, near Whitby craftsman. The work included the woodcarver's signature, a small gnome, perhaps a reminder of Hoppity.

1969 Rounders team with Jean Lumb

Recorder group 1970 with Jeanne Loxam

Centenary Year 1969
Pictured at the launch
of the first edition of
The Story of a School
are *from the left:*
Norman Lister,
Canon Frank White,
Geoff Hudson,
John Brooke and
Colin Johnson.

**Kitchen and lunchtime
supervisory staff 1970.**
Included here are: Joyce Clarke,
Barbara Horner, June Jennings,
Mavis Martin, Marian Nield,
Phyllis Redfearn, Joyce Scott,
Mabel Sheard, Margaret Sibary.

**1976 netball team with
Jackie Nobbs**

Canon White leaves the parish, March 1972
Staff and pupils gather to say goodbye to the vicar who was leaving to become the vicar of
Leathley with Farnley.

Staff 1972
From the left, back: Pat Hartley, Margaret Whitaker, Betty Carney, Jean Dobson, Margaret Hudson,
Catherine Styan, Madge Laycock, Jackie Nobbs. *Front:* Elizabeth Beaumont, Kathryn Jowitt,
Jeanne O'Rourke, Christopher Wood, Norman Lister, Robert Leeming, Susan Cawkwell,
Jean Lumb, Jeannette McPhail

Norman Lister. Headteacher 1968-83

It was also during Norman Lister's headship, in 1974, that local government reorganisation placed the school under the jurisdiction of the new local education authority, Calderdale and the West Riding County Council was consigned to history. The headquarters of the WRCC were based in Wakefield but the local office was at the Manor House in Brighouse situated just below the library and the former Brighouse Girls' Grammar School. The WRCC, one of the country's foremost education authorities, had been created under the terms of the 1902 Education Act. From that date until 1944 the school had also been under the guidance of the minor Brighouse Education Authority. Former pupils will remember the WRCC initials appearing on virtually every piece of equipment even the smallest of items: pencils, rulers, drawing pins and every sheet of toilet paper!

Although the local authority's scheme for selection at eleven continued for another decade local government reorganisation meant the end of pupils transferring at eleven to West Riding County Council Grammar Schools outside the Brighouse area. (Halifax secondary schools were not, until 1974, available, to Lightcliffe pupils). 1972 saw the final pupils from Lightcliffe—Jane Harrison, Sandra Lister (later captain of the England Ladies' Hockey team and a member of the national ladies' cricket team), Amanda Stead and Karen Whiteley, transfer to Whitcliffe Mount Grammar School in Cleckheaton. As it was, the school became a 13-18 comprehensive school the following year, when selection ended in the Spen Valley. That same year, in addition to the local grammar school choices of Hipperholme and Rastrick for boys, and Brighouse for girls, seven pupils transferred to Sowerby Bridge Grammar School. Whitcliffe Mount School had always been a popular co-educational option for Lightcliffe pupils especially in the 1950s. Those attending will remember the crowded additional service buses that were provided by the Yorkshire Woollen District company and how the ascent of Birkby Lane beyond Bailiff Bridge proved just too much for them. On many occasions pupils had to disembark and walk alongside the bus as it crawled up the steep hill.

The following logbook extracts will give readers a further picture of the many school events during this period.

8 October 1968
A presentation was made to Mrs Hartley of the school meals staff, on completion of 25 years' service at the school.

3 March 1969
Mrs Madge Laycock commenced duties as clerical assistant.

25 April 1969
A cheese and wine evening was held in school to mark the centenary of the school and the launching of the history of the school. Amongst many friends, we were pleased to welcome Mr GL Armitage, Miss Ethel Womersley and Miss A Dyson a previous head of Hipperholme Infants' School who is now 90 years old.

30 October 1969
Brooke's Chemicals demolished five chimneys. The event was witnessed by the children at lunchtime.

18 June 1971
Television set received at school.

7 April 1972
A football team from Callington School, Cornwall visited school to play a game which resulted in a four-all draw.

1 March 1973
A presentation was made to Mrs Sheard who is leaving tomorrow after 23 years' service in the school kitchen.

17 March 1975
The school had a float in the Whitsuntide Walk procession. The event was in connection with the church centenary.

27 January 1976
Mrs Cawkwell's class visited Clarke Hall, Wakefield built in 1680. The children dressed in period costume.

26 November 1977
School won the indoor five-a-side football competition at Eastfield School. Nineteen schools took part.

Library official opening 1977
From the left: Mrs J Dowson, Mrs M Bullough, RN Lister, C Johnson, The Revd MGS Whitcombe,
Mrs J Heap, Mrs J Widdop
This extension is now part of the visitors' entrance area at the eastern end of the foundation building.

8 January 1979
A colour television set was installed in place of the monochrome set.

30 August 1979
A managers' meeting was held with the supervisor of caretakers, Mr Shields, present.
Mr Brian Moore was appointed to the vacant post.

7 December 1979
The Bishop of Wakefield, the Right Reverend Colin James, visited school.

13 February 1982
The Calderdale chess jamboree was held in school. 150 children took part.

7 May 1983
Victorian May Fair held on the school field. Despite three heavy downpours over
£1600 was raised by the committee.

27 June 1983
Parents from Norwood Green School (closure announced today) came to look round
school.

26 November 1983
Parents' and friends' outing to London, organised by the Building Fund Committee.

Class group with Jeanne O'Rourke 1983

Staff 1983
From the left. Back: Valerie Deadman, Elaine Bates, Jennifer Brooke, Dorothy Taylor, Margaret Whitaker.
Middle: Robert Kinghorn, Maria Ingleheart, Barbara Horsman, Madge Llaycock, Jeannette McPhail,
Jackie Nobbs. *Front:* Pauline Marshall, Alan Rhodes, Norman Lister, Colin Woods, Jeanne O'Rouke.

Class group with Alan Rhodes 1983

Class group with Jeanette McPhail 1985

Staff gather for Norman Lister's farewell evening in 1983

The Revd David Wilding shakes the retiring headteacher's hand watched by, unless indicated, teaching staff. At the back from the left: Barbara Horsman, Colin Woods, Jennifer Brooke, Pauline Marshall, Jeanette McPhail, Madge Laycock (secretary) Alan Rhodes, Brian Moore. (caretaker). *At the front from the left:* Elaine Bates, Jeanne O'Rourke, Valerie Deadman, Anita Hankinson, Margaret Whitaker, Jackie Nobbs.

Chapter Eight

Towards One Hundred and Twenty-five Years

The governors appointed your author as successor to Norman Lister in May 1983 and I commenced duties in the following January. Prior to becoming head at Lightcliffe I had been head of Kirkheaton County Primary School from its opening in 1972. Like my immediate predecessor I had also begun my teaching career at Lightcliffe, in my case just over twenty years earlier. During the 1983 autumn term the school was led by Colin Woods who had been deputy headteacher since 1973, when Robert Leeming left to become head at Lepton CE School.

It was during the autumn term1983, that work began on the extensions already referred to here. There was inevitably more disruption to the life of the school but the contractors, Longdens, completed the work by the beginning of the autumn term 1984. The three extra classrooms, at the west end of the school, were especially welcome as was the new kitchen where, for the first time in the school's history, meals were cooked on the premises. The governing body had at last, after initially raising the issue some forty years previously, been granted their wish! There was also additional hard-surface playing area following the removal of the mobile units. More extensions were to follow during the early 1990s.

Inevitably the story of a school cannot isolate itself from the local or national scene. This had been a recurring theme throughout the school's history and continues to this day. In 1928, for example, major plans had been drawn up for the reorganisation of elementary schools in the Brighouse area and Lightcliffe School was to lose its senior (11-14) pupils. Two major decisions, the reorganisation of secondary education in the Brighouse area and the closure of Hipperholme Infants' School impacted on the school during the 1980s.

It was from the beginning of the 1985 school year that the secondary education system in Brighouse was finally reorganised after almost thirty years of debate and fluctuating opinions. Around twelve months earlier the Education Secretary, Sir Keith Joseph, had agreed with the proposals for the area put forward by the local authority. Selection at eleven was to end and three new comprehensive schools were to be created: Brighouse High School (initially using the Brighouse Girls' Grammar school building in the town and the annexe at Slead Syke), Hipperholme and Lightcliffe High School on the Eastfield Secondary School site, and Rastrick High School, an amalgamation of Rastrick Grammar School and Reins Wood Secondary School, on the latter site although initially the grammar school buildings were retained as an annexe.

Staff 1985

From the left. Back: Derrick Rooke, Jim Ogden, John Brooke,, Colin Woods, Robert Kinghorn.
Centre: Student, Jeannette McPhail, Barbara Horsman, Maria Ingleheart, Valerie Deadman,
Marion Hoyle, Student.
Front; Jeanne O'Rourke, Anita Hankinson, Margaret Whitaker, Student, Pauline Marshall,
Elaine Bates, Madge Laycock.

Class group with Ruth Paxman 1990

The governors of Hipperholme Grammar School chose to remain outside the system and the school is now an independent grammar school. The system in the former County Borough of Halifax remained unchanged at this stage. A non-selective system was introduced in 1992 but without the involvement of the Grant-Maintained grammar schools of Crossley Heath and North Halifax (initially Highlands).

During the late 1960s a middle school system for the Brighouse area had been agreed upon by the WRCC and at one stage Lightcliffe was pencilled in as a 9-13 middle school. New middle schools were built at Slead Syke (the buildings are now part of Brighouse High School) and at Carr Green. A new 5-9 first school was built in Rastrick and is now Castlefields Infants' School. These plans were never implemented owing to long-standing differing points of view amongst the Church, the governors of the aided grammar schools and the local authority, centred around the 13-18 high schools. Two new secondary school had already been built for the 13-18 age group, at Eastfield and Reins Wood but only ever operated as secondary modern schools. Additionally the demise of the WRCC in 1974 did not help to move the plans forward.

The second key event, and one that impacted more directly on this school was the closure of Hipperholme Infants' school in 1990. The church school at Hipperholme had, as we have heard, been closely associated with Lightcliffe since its opening in 1885. It was in 1883 that the Education department had issued an order which stated that additional school accommodation had to be provided for the Hipperholme area, to cater for 180 children, or steps would be taken to form a school board. At a meeting in the National School on 12 November, with John Lister of Shibden Hall in the chair, a decision was made to erect a church school, initially for infants and standard one pupils, near the crossroads and so release the township from the addition of a school rate. A subscription list was drawn up to pay for the building and this was headed, with £150, by the Lancashire and Yorkshire Railway Company, followed by well over 100 names. A total of £1,400 3s 6d was raised that, after the work was completed, left a balance of £14 13s 3d.

It was during the late 1980s that the local authority began to have serious discussions with the governors of the Hipperholme School where only 38 pupils were on roll. The plans became public knowledge on 3 March 1989 when, following speculation in the *Brighouse Echo* the deputy chief education officer, Peter Edmondson, confirmed the news. Notices were published the following August indicating that the LEA intended to cease to maintain Hipperholme CE Controlled Infants' School. The secretary of state supported the plan and the school closed in 1990 at the end of the summer term. A service to commemorate the work of the school was held in St Matthew's Church on 6 July. A tree was planted in the Lightcliffe grounds by Doreen Unwin, the Hipperholme School headteacher, who in turn had received gifts and good wishes form the Hipperholme School Chairman of Governors, Councillor Chris O'Connor.

The Hipperholme building did, however, have one more year as a school when it reopened in late August as an annexe to Lightcliffe School as building work had not yet begun to extend the school. History was repeating itself as rooms at Hipperholme Methodist Church had, as we have already heard, been used by Lightcliffe pupils during the first phase of extensions in 1966. A single age group of Year 6 pupils spent twelve months in the building with teachers Colin Woods, the deputy head, Sarah Thomson and Nicola Dunkley. In turn a number of the Hipperholme staff transferred to Lightcliffe: teachers Janet Thomas, Joan Burchill and a number of support staff. Doreen Unwin retired and Shirley Lawton, who had worked in the kitchen for 17 years, transferred to St Andrew's Infants' School in 1991.

Work on the extensions to create a purpose-built early years' block began in April 1991. The visionary plans had been drawn up by the Abbey Hanson Rowe partnership and the contractors were FN Allman of Leeds. The extensions, which cost around £250,000, were officially opened by the Bishop of Wakefield, the Right Reverend Nigel McCulloch on 9 May 1992. Prior to the opening ceremony all the 200 guests had gathered in the school hall where the chairman of governors, the Reverend David Wilding, welcomed everyone and introduced the guest speaker, Mrs Jackie Tongue, Calderdale Director of Education designate.

The major national issue during the period covered by this chapter, was the 1988 Education Reform Act which resulted in the most important legislation since 1944. It was not immediately universally popular. However, the introduction of the national curriculum, a key element, was basically accepted and supported by the teaching profession especially after its initial somewhat overpowering demands were slimmed down.

There was also the opportunity for the school to become self-governing. Following a ballot of the parents, which the governors instigated, the school left the local authority and became Grant Maintained from 1 January 1995. This was, in a sense, a

The official opening of the reception classes' unit, 1992
Miss Jackie Tongue (Calderdale Director of Education), John Brooke, Mrs Jennifer Brooke,
The Rt. Revd. Nigel McCulloch, (Bishop of Wakefield) , Mrs Frances Thompson (Deputy Mayoress),
Andrew Thompson (Deputy Mayor), Mrs Denise Shields (Acting Deputy Headteacher),
The Revd David Wilding (Chair of governors), Mrs Brenda Wilding.

**The school orchestra at the opening ceremony 1992
with Sarah Thomson and Margaret Whitaker**

Staff 1996
Standing from the left: Andrew Inns, Jean Pidgeon, Maria Ingleheart, Tracey Richardson, Janet Thomas, Catherine MacDonald, Philip Knowles, Marion Hoyle, Jeanne O'Rourke. *Seated back:* Joanna Blackburn, John Brooke, Margaret Whitaker. *Middle:* Julie Batty, Kathryn Rushby, Samantha Keitch, Jane Beaumont, Rachel Brooke. *Front two rows from left:* Elizabeth Whittaker, Joanna Woodward, Denise Shields, Derrick Rooke, Sarah Brown, Joan Burchill, Jim Ogden, Ruth Paxman.

return to pre-1902 days, before the Balfour Act created local authorities, when schools received central government funding. The school remained part of the Wakefield Diocesan Council for Education and continued to use many of the services of the Calderdale Education Department with whom it remained on good terms.

Before we look briefly at events during this time recorded in the logbooks a few events do, perhaps, warrant recording in a little more detail. These include the continuing success of the chess teams and the sports' teams, the further development of the grounds as an educational resource, the growth of the school orchestra, and the continuation of the educational visits.

In June 1984 and again in 1987, the school's under-nine chess team, as north of England champions, were invited to London to play a London School in the Teachers' Assurance Championships. Unfortunately, they were beaten on both occasions. Individual pupils had success, however, and in 1985 Caroline Millichope was the national girls' under-eight champion.

The checkmate champions

CHESS stars from Lightcliffe Church of England School have reached the final of a national competition for primary schools.

The team, all aged nine and under, have won the northern section of a team competition organised by the English Primary Schools Chess Association.

The contest trail started when Lightcliffe beat Horbury Bridge School from Wakefield by 5-0. They then went on to beat Hightown Church of England 3½-1½, and Castle Hill School, Todmorden 4-1. In the quarter-finals they travelled to King Street Primary in County Durham to win by 3½-1½, and the knocked out Blackburn school Rishton Methodists 4-1 in the semis.

In the northern final they beat St Alban's Primary School from Kings Heath, Birmingham at home on a board count after the two teams drew 2½-2½ on five games. The tie hinged on the first four games and Lightcliffe won by 2½-1½.

The team is pictured here from the left: Matthew Greenwood (9), Christopher Parker (9), Andrew Waddington (8), Richard Oliver (8), Michael Brooke (8) and Frank Ralph (8). Not on the picture are squad members Jamie Farrell and John Carter.

☐ MEMBERS of the Lightcliffe Church of England School under-nine chess team who have reached the final of a national competition

The under-nine chess team reach the national finals 1984 *(The Brighouse Echo)*

The school orchestra was formed in 1984 and was led by part-time teacher Margaret Whitaker who had over the years also developed the school choir to a particularly high standard. A wide range of tuition was provided by visiting Calderdale instrumental teachers. The school also had, during this period, a number of members of the teaching staff with musical ability and they often joined the twenty-five or so pupils in the school orchestra.

Margaret Whitaker retired in July 1996 after twenty-five years' service. This was a period in the school's history that also saw the retirement of three other long-serving members of the teaching staff: Jeannette McPhail in 1991 and Valerie Deadman in 1994, both after 19 years at the school, and Jacqueline Nobbs after 25 years in 1995.

The residential visits, already referred to, continued during this period. The activities were very much as they always had been: walking, town and village studies, shoreline and woodland observations. The events experienced were recorded in detail in the pupils' diaries. Comments provided the reader with an eclectic mix of the educational element of the visit and a review of the social aspects, as the following indicate following a Whitby visit:

In St Mary's Church there is a three-decker pulpit which is not seen in other churches. There are two ear trumpets at the side as one of the vicars had a wife who was partially deaf.

We thought the hotel was very nice. What we didn't like was all the steps as they were very tiring to walk up.

Events recorded in the school logbook during the period 1984-97 include

4 April 1984
It was agreed at a Building Fund Committee meeting that the organisation should be renamed the 'Development Association'.

13 July 1984
63 children leave today and transfer, after the holidays, to 17 different schools!

13 December 1985
Three of our pupils who won the Calderdale 'Write a Carol Competition' (Helen Barry, Rachel Turner and Rachel Wood) received their award at a carol service in the Brighouse Civic Hall Theatre.

Write a Carol Competition winners 1985
From the left: Rachel Wood, Rachel Turner and Helen Barry
(The Halifax Courier)

2 October 1986
Mr Woods's and Mr Kinghorn's classes visited the plague village of Eyam in Derbyshire.

9 June 1987
Our orchestra and choir entertained throughout the afternoon at Councillor Sharp's 'Mayor at Home' held at Lightcliffe United Reformed Church.

6 November 1987
A school pond and seating area was dedicated today by the Revd David Wilding, in memory of Mrs Elaine Bates, a member of staff, who died the previous Easter. Derrick Rooke had led the project assisted by a group of parents.

Learning beyond the classroom
A group with Derrick Rooke in 1986, when the school was involved in a research project with Leicester University and Trinity and All Saints' College.

A visit to Eyam 1986.
Colin Woods and pupils taking a rubbing of the table-top grave of Catherine Mompesson, the rector's wife, who was one of the victims of the plague.

Computer studies 1988
Robert Cooper and David Bottomley with one of the school's early desk-top computers

4 December 1987
105 of our children were involved in the official welcome for Prince Charles when he inaugurated the Children's Museum (Eureka Project) in Halifax. He spoke to many of them.

21 June 1988
Representatives of the Gideons were in school for the first time to present Bibles to those leaving us for secondary education.

6 May 1991
The Prince of Wales met teacher Ruth Paxman and three former pupils. They had, whilst with us, produced under Mrs Paxman's guidance, a mural for the Brighouse Market Hall.

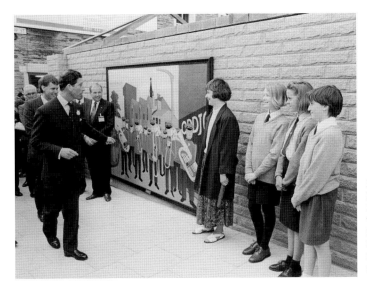

Prince Charles in Brighouse 1991
Prince Charles speaking with Ruth Paxman and former pupils (from the left) Nicola Merriman, Laura Smith and Katie Green
(The Brighouse Echo)

20 March 1993

The Development Association (initially the Building Fund Committee) celebrated its 40th anniversary with a dance in the school hall. Guests included Mrs Kathleen Briggs, a founder member, who cut a special cake.

Anniversary party is a winner

CELEBRATIONS went with a swing at Lightcliffe Church of England School when a party was held to mark the 40th anniversary of the school's Development Association.

The group was formed in February 1953 by St Matthew's Church, Lightcliffe and has helped the school with financing four extensions plus other work.

A cake, depicting the school badge, was made for the occasion by Mrs Jean Firth, who has a grandchild at the school, and a hot supper was prepared by school cook Mrs Janet Moran.

The work of the association was explained by its chairman, Mr David Smith, and the school head, Mr John Brooke, explained how the association had helped the school.

Chairman of the school governors, the Rev David Wilding, expressed his thanks to the association for its support.

Members of staff and parents got together to form a seven piece band and there was also entertainment from a vocalist.

Pictured at the event are, from the left, Mr Smith, Mrs Jane Turner, a parent and committee member, Mrs Doreen Worsick, a former committee member, the Rev Wilding, Mrs Valerie Deadman, secretary of the association and a member of staff, Mrs Kathleen Briggs, a founder member, and Mr Brooke.

Kathleen Briggs (née Hartley) is also shown as a pupil, front row third from left, on p.24.
(The Brighouse Echo)

18 November 1994

Measles injection day. As part of a national campaign virtually every child received an anti-measles injection. Some eight nurses and a doctor were in attendance.

16 December 1994

Mrs Madge Laycock, the school secretary for over 25 years, retired today.

10 January 1996

The staff (teaching and support) plus the governing body (60 people in total) dined out at Crow Nest Golf Club. A special presentation was made to Mrs Peggy Scott who retires shortly as a school governor after 20 years' service.

Work begins during the holidays to create a large staffroom in the roof void of the central section of the foundation building.

16 January 1997

The second edition of *The Story of a School* was launched with 'wine and food' at a special event in the evening.

5 March 1997

We received an 'Investor in People' award that deputy head Catherine MacDonald had worked hard to achieve for the school, at a presentation evening at the McAlpine Stadium in Huddersfield.

The six-side football team reach the Refuge Assurance northern final at York 1995.
Teacher Tim Freeman with, *from the left,* Scott Rooks, Robert Kenny, Edward Hennessy, James Flower,
Michael Lund, Ben Whiteley, Matthew Baxter, James Parkinson, Simon Naylor, Luke Parker.
(Courtesy Halifax Town AFC)

23 May 1997

A new flag pole was dedicated today by the Reverend David Wilding in memory of
Matthew Edward Brooke. Almost 54 years to the day since the original pole was
erected in memory of another old scholar, Ethel Hayles.

My final day at the school was 18 July 1997 and one week earlier there had been a
retirement evening for me. 180 guests gathered including present and former
colleagues, my friends and family, parents, governors, Calderdale staff and musicians
from the Calderdale Music Centre. Patrick Beeson, the chairman of governors, acted
as master of ceremonies.

We now move on to another era following my retirement and the appointment of
Anthony (Tony) Berwick as head teacher. He was, at the time of his appointment,
headteacher of West Vale Primary School.

Chapter Nine

1998-2019: The Headships of Anthony Berwick and Charles Woodbridge

Tony Berwick struck an encouraging note on his first day at the school when he recorded that 'all the teaching staff made me feel very welcome' and how noticeable the 'calm and purposeful atmosphere' was. His first assembly included a sombre note as the whole school reflected on the recent death of Diana, Princess of Wales. Four weeks later the headteacher was in Whitby, after clearly an early start, to have breakfast with the Lightcliffe pupils and staff (Jim Ogden, Christine Kemp and Marion Hoyle) there. It was a lovely autumn day and the pupils were clearly enjoying themselves, recorded Tony Berwick. A few days earlier teachers Derrick Rooke, Tracey Richardson and Susan Fox had been there with the other half of the year group.

Later in the 1997 autumn term the school developed links with Kassell in Germany and two teachers from there visited Lightcliffe as did two from Finland who were on the same scheme. The school was continuing with a long-standing tradition and the head was regularly welcoming visits from individuals or groups to the school. There were more visitors in school at the beginning of 1998 when the school's first Ofsted inspection took place. There had, of course, been many HMI inspections of the school over the years but this was the beginning of a revised system. Happily, the school was judged to be 'good, with many strengths'. There had been good news too in the Berwick household, just a week earlier, when the head's wife gave birth to twin girls: Lucy and Sarah.

1998 was, in fact, proving to be a busy year for the headteacher and the governors following the passing of the School Standards and Framework Act. The key points of the act, in relation to the school, were the imposing of a limit of 30 in infant classes and the abolition of grant-maintained schools. It was not long before there were meetings regarding the school's future status and Tony Berwick and Stanley Coulton, the chairman of governors, attended a meeting in October to hear about the process of returning the school to aided status. On the 19 November the governors voted unanimously to do just that. By December the restriction on numbers was already causing some concern amongst parents and the headteacher met with a number of them. The school was already over subscribed by 24. The lack of availability of places regularly caused some problems for the school as it did, noted the head, for so-called 'parental choice' at secondary level. The school revised its admissions policy in April 2003 with a view to alleviating some of the problems that had occurred.

Tony Berwick recalls the many events and functions held during his time in office ranging from concerts, productions such as *Bugsy Malone*, *Cinders* and *The Rocky Monster Show* charity fundraising events, book weeks and poetry competition success. In November 1999 the school was invited to take part in the BBC's *Songs of Praise* programme and the children were filmed rehearsing a Nativity play. The performers met, and were photographed with, the presenter and former 'Coronation Street' actress Debbie McAndrew.

Technology was also increasing at a pace and the head was to the forefront of the many advances. During his time at the school a splendid computer room was established and the school played host to Calderdale training day led by the headteacher who was also, later in 2000, seconded part-time to manage the 'Calderdale Teachers for the Future Project'. Earlier on 13 July 1998 the head was clearly pleased to record that 'two laptop computers were delivered for the special needs co-ordinator and me. Email here we come'.

On 28 April 2003 Tony Berwick announced that he would be leaving at the end of term to take up the position of headteacher at a school in Germany. A leaving event was arranged for staff and governors in early July. Around two weeks later the headteacher recorded that there was a good attendance at a parents' open evening. He must have very pleased to note that it was a 'very pleasant evening—no complaints at all'! A happy note, then, on which to end his term of office at the school.

There were other staff departures in addition to the headteacher's. Teacher FH (Jim) Ogden was retiring after 19 years at the school, and support staff Carolyn Bretton and Helen Wood (who later returned to the school as a member of the teaching staff) were leaving for 'new jobs and careers'. The longest serving member of the staff leaving was Mavis Rothwell who had worked in the school kitchen for 22 years, and before that for five years at Norwood Green School immediately prior to its closure.

Class group with Tim Feeman 1993

Class group with Julie Asquith c1999

Class group with Samantha Keitch and Jane Beaumont 2001

Class group with Tracey Richardson 1998

Staff 2002
From left. Back row: Diane Thornton, Derrick Rooke, Kelly Bourne, Jane Beaumont, Joan Burchill.
Middle row: Ruth Paxman, Julie Asquith, Janet Thomas, Katy Cooper, Elaine Maycock, Jeanne O'Rourke,
Christine Kemp. *Front row:* Rachel Brooke, Sarah Brown, Catherine MacDonald, Tony Berwick,
Denise Shields, Jim Ogden, Marion Hoyle.

Entires in the logbook during this period include:

14 November 1997
PC Wareing from the British Transport Police spoke to Key Stage 2 pupils about safety near railway lines.

9 June 1998
Year 5 visited the new mosque in Gibbet Street, Halifax

12 June 1998
Mrs Jo Woodward, school administrator, left us today. She is succeeded by Mrs Jean Pidgeon.

27 November 1998
Norman Lister and John Brooke (former headteachers) in school for an 'historic picture' taken using our digital camera.

Headteachers 1969-2003
From left: John Brooke, Tony Berwick and Norman Lister in 1998

7 December 1998
Fire escape from the staffroom finally completed, at a cost of £12,000

10 February 1999
Halifax Building Society use the school for an advert – a giant X

27 September 1999
Governors' meeting. It was decided to formally adopt grey trousers as part of the girls' uniform.

30 March 2000
A visit from a Mr O'Grady [Kenneth it is now believed] who was an evacuee from Hull during the war, and came to the school in 1944.

8 May 2000
Bishop Nigel arrived to talk to the whole school. He presented a wooden cross to celebrate the new millennium.

In June 2003 it was announced that Tony Berwick would be succeeded by Charles Woodbridge, the headteacher of Gomersal CE School. His appointment took effect from the beginning of 2004, so for the autumn term school was led by Catherine MacDonald, the deputy head.

Soon after Charles Woodbridge's arrival there were building matters to attend to when the kitchen was completely refurbished. There were other matters too such as the complete renovation of the foundation building's slate roof that cost £440,000 and the replacement of the windows at a cost of £60,000. This work was not only essential but was done sensitively to the highest standard preserving the fine building for the future. There was, however, unwanted and unplanned work at the end of 2010 when a large water tank in the loft burst during inclement weather and some classrooms at the eastern end of the school could not be occupied until Easter. In 2012 the teaching staff were pleased to learn that, following new and larger fire doors, the whole school could once again meet together in the hall.

Teaching staff and some members of the support staff 2006
From left. Back row: Debbie Simpson, Lois Moss, Catherine Stansfield, Charlotte Scott, Althea Rhodes. *Middle row:* Christine Halernik, Claire Duffield, Carol Brown, Kelly Bourne, Ruth Paxman, Helen Austin, Louise Brennan, Jane Beaumont, Samantha Keitch, Monique Millar, Derrick Rooke, Katrina Thomas, Joanna Blackburn, Helen Wood, Chris Watson Jill Hartley, Margaret Bottomley, Pat Wood. Carol Brown. *Front row:* Helen Bell, Rachel Brooke, Sarah Brown, Catherine MacDonald, Charles Woodbridge, Denise Shields, Kate Dunkley, Brian Moore.

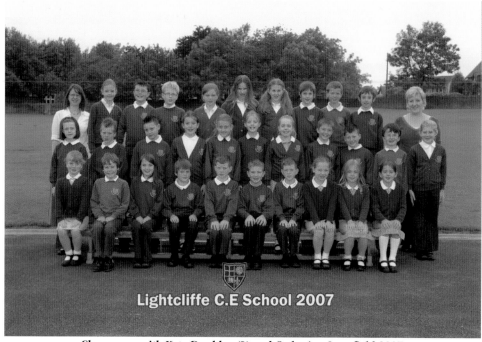

Class group with Kate Dunkley (L) and Catherine Stansfield 2007

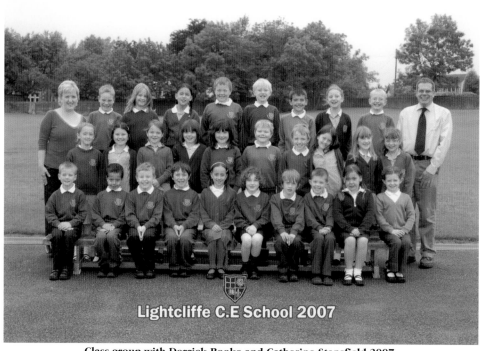

Class group with Derrick Rooke and Catherine Stansfield 2007

The curriculum continued to develop and was, as ever, supported by a wide range of visitors and visits. The residential visits, established over 50 years ago, have continued and currently the destinations are Whitby, for year six, and Robinwood at Todmorden for year five. Following a visit to Whitby in 2011 staff and pupils would have been delighted to learn that the bus driver had written to the headteacher praising most highly the excellent behaviour of the children. Parents were keen to hear of any current educational developments and in 2003 a 'Helping your child with literacy and maths' evening was so successful that parents asked for more! By 2005 there was a smart-board in each classroom. Exactly 100 years earlier the headteacher had recorded that 'slates are quite abandoned' in most year groups and little used in others.

The children were, as ever, encouraged to think of the wider community, be it local, national or global. Catherine MacDonald remembers that throughout her long career at Lightcliffe there were many targeted fund-raising events following, for example, international tragedies such as earthquakes and famine, and this philosophy continues to be encouraged.

The school's link with Mara in East Africa has been, and continues to be, the outstanding example of this. This grew out of the link that had been established in 1985 by St Matthew's Church and the Wakefield Diocese with the Nyamatare parish in Tanzania. It was in 2001 that the headteacher of Mara Primary School, Nyamatare visited school and the relationship was forged. School began fundraising and the children started to learn about life in an African village. The first fundraising project was to buy desks and books for the school there. Further projects supported the establishment of a new toilet block and a fence for the school compound to keep the animals out.

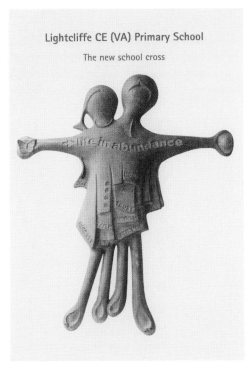

Lightcliffe CE (VA) Primary School

The new school cross

In 2005 deputy headteacher Catherine MacDonald visited Mara as a member of the Diocesan team. She taught in all the classes, worked alongside the teachers and wrote the school development plan alongside the headteacher and staff. She returned in 2010 along with members of St Matthew's Church, Ernest and Dorothy Gelder, and Jean Lumb. Since her retirement she has made two further visits, in 2013 and 2015.

The new school cross
The cross, designed by Graham Alcock, was dedicated at a special ceremony in June 2016 by the Bishop of Leeds, Nick Baines

In 2011 the Lister wing, named after the late Norman Lister, was opened by his widow, Molly. This splendid addition was developed out of the former school house that had for many years been occupied by the school caretaker, and the adjacent small upstairs classroom. There is a library, ICT suite and facilities for the out of school club. A considerable sum of money had been raised by the parents and friends group, and Mrs Lister wrote to the headteacher expressing her appreciation of the whole project. Norman, she said, 'would have been delighted with the whole transformation of that part of the building'.

One of the highlights of 2013 was the staff pantomime that followed a successful Ofsted Inspection. Those who worked in the school buildings were supported by staff associated with, but not directly employed by, the school. One example was Richard Varley, the long-serving and popular crossing-patrol attendant, who starred as the dame. Perhaps there was a sense of relief on the part of the staff as they 'let their hair down' following a 'good across all aspects' report with standards in key subjects all above average. The children enjoyed both the pantomime and the letter that they had received from the inspection team. They were told that they attended a good school and the lead inspector concluded by adding 'I am pleased that you are proud of your school, and I wish you well for the future'.

A year later there was a lunchtime picnic to celebrate the Queen's Golden Jubilee with everyone dressed in red, white and blue. The school chef Paul Tyler (Mr Paul) and his team prepared a splendid street-party meal. There was an exhibition of artwork by the children and each child was presented with a commemorative mug.

Over the years, as we have seen, the school has been blessed with many long-serving members of both teaching and non-teaching staff. The retirement of many of them has been noted throughout this book. It is perhaps, though, the last decade that has seen the retirement of the majority of those who have worked at the school for many years. Two teachers, particularly, served the school for remarkably long periods and merit more than a passing mention. Jeanne O'Rourke joined the staff in January 1969 and retired after 37 years and one term's service in March 2005. For much of that time she was a senior member of staff and led the what is now key-stage one team. Derrick Rooke began in September 1983 and retired in 2018 after 35 years at the school. During his time at Lightcliffe he contributed much to the development of the school grounds as a learning resource. Both gave outstanding service to the school and their time here was exceeded only by Ethel Womersley's 45 years and Kathleen Kaye's, 40.

Other particularly long-serving members of the teaching staff who retired during this time were Ruth Paxman (26 years) Marion Hoyle (29 years) and Denise Shields (21 years, many as assistant headteacher). Three current members of staff, Jane Beaumont, Samantha Blackhurst and Rachel Brooke who began their careers at the school are currently (August 2019) still teaching at the school after, respectively, 30, 29 and 28 years.

Catherine MacDonald, who was deputy headteacher for twenty years and worked alongside three headteachers, retired in 2012 after twenty years at the school. She joined the staff from Bailiff Bridge School in August 1992 following the retirement of Colin Woods. In a governors' report at the time of her retirement Charles Woodbridge noted that she was 'held in high esteem by all who work with her, and the wider school community'. Catherine MacDonald was replaced as deputy head by Kate Dunkley, who had joined the staff in 2003.

It was not only long-serving members of the teaching staff that left the school during this period. Brian Moore who was appointed as caretaker in September 1979, retired in December 2016 after over 37 years at the school. His role expanded over the years as supervisor of the premises and grounds' manager. He worked with four headteachers and had served the school and the community with distinction. No one could have done more for the school.

There were also departures of long-serving support staff during this period. Andrea Petch retired in October 1999 after 21 years as a kitchen assistant, Mavis Wood in 2004 after over 15 years as senior lunchtime supervisor, Norma Hill in 2002 after 21 years as assistant caretaker and, initially, as caretaker at Hipperholme Infants' School, Rita Mason in 2017 who for 23 years was a mid-day supervisor and later cleaner, and June Bell, in 2019, after over 20 years as a lunchtime supervisor. Elizabeth Field, kitchen staff assistant and then cleaner, and Althea Rhodes, mid-day supervisor and cleaner, who both began in 1995 are currently still working at the school. Helen Bell who joined the staff as school administrator in 2002 still manages the school office as business manger.

School governors have also, over the years, served the school for long periods. Names such as Robert Goldthorp, Colin Johnson, Peggy Scott, Pat Beeson and Stanley Longbottom immediately spring to mind. Perhaps, though, no governor has done more for the school than Michael Wood who is still a member of the governing body some 35 years after being appointed.

By 2004 the school's grant-maintained status had been scrapped, following decisions at national level and the school returned to local authority control. However, in 2017 the governors decided to accept the government's opportunity to become an academy and joined a multi-academy trust. We wrote in 1969 that education was a maelstrom of ideas and that it was increasingly difficult to 'foresee developments even in the immediate future'. During the past 50 years this has proved to be the case, the changes in the school's status being just one example. The introduction of the local comprehensive system, a nationally imposed curriculum, standard assessment tasks and regular Ofsted inspections are other initiatives.

Whatever the future holds for the school one thing is sure. It is still, as Sutherland Walker wished, a Church of England School. It is still a school that is very much part of the local community and one which has, as already indicated, educated generations of local people. It is a school that fulfils the expectations that the founder expressed at the opening ceremony 150 years ago. We can now look back with pride at its long history, from a time when universal elementary education was merely an aspiration, to the present day when all have the opportunity to be educated. Despite all the changes and the developments, a key aim of all associated with the school is clearly, that the children 'might have life and have it more abundantly'.

Afterword

Schools, whether small rural ones or large inner-city ones, are a vital part of our communities. Churches also, have a similar role to play as enduring institutions within every community in this country. When the two work well together, all members of the community can benefit. Looking at the 150 year history of Lightcliffe CE Primary School, I think this is why the school was founded and what it, and the church, have worked towards since the beginning.

Education and nurture are life-giving and life-enhancing and our society would be greatly impoverished if we were denied either of these. Both church and school do their best to provide education and nurture for the community. It is clear from this history of the school that many people have fond memories of school and recognise the contribution it has made to the community. St Matthew's church is also very grateful to the school for all that it has brought to church life over the years. Church schools embody the notion of 'partnership', where both parties benefit from, and enjoy, a collaborative relationship.

On reading these pages it is clear that there have, of course, been many changes in education. What strikes me, though, is that much of this history is about people and their experiences, dedication and commitment. People make up the history of this school and they deserve our thanks and appreciation for how they have enriched the life of this community from 1869 to the present day. Let us all hope that schools will be enabled to continue their good work so that children in generations to come might, indeed, 'have life and have it more abundantly' and that Lightcliffe Primary C E School will hold fast to its foundation as a community church school.

Kathryn Buck, Vicar of Lightcliffe
November 2019

Class group with Emily Langhorn and Rachael Ho 2015

Staff of 2019

Lightcliffe CE Primary School

The school staff 2019

From left to right: Mrs N. Eliasz, Mr P. Tyler, Miss N. Brown, Mrs S. Coldwell, Mrs J. Beaumont, Mrs G. Gillespie, Mr C.R.V. Woodbridge, Mrs S. Blackhurst, Mrs R. Brooke, Mrs H. Wood, Mrs E. Langhorn, Mrs C. Stephenson, Mrs A. Brunkard, Mrs C. Stansfield, Mrs J. Jackson. Mrs C. Watson, Mrs A. Hemingway, Mrs P. Clarke, Mrs M. Brook, Miss B. Stephenson, Mrs B. O'Rourke, Mrs A. Greenwood, Mrs H. Bell, Mrs L. Dukes, Mr C. Wildgust, Mrs A. Hustler, Miss K. Bourne, Mrs R. Ho, Miss R. Parkinson, Mrs L. Moss, Mrs L. Webb.Mrs M. McDonald, Mrs R. Schoon, Mrs J. Ball, Mrs G. Gregg, Mrs D. Swift and Mrs K. Todd.

(Image courtesy of H Tempest Ltd, staff details courtesy of the school)

Appendices

1. Headteachers

Boys' School

John O Rusholme	1869-1873
William Cook	1873-1890
J Robert Markham	1890-1894
George G Hague	1898-1906

Girls' School

Mary L Drake	1869-1882
Mary E Fairbrother	1882-1887
Mary Clubbs	1887-1891
Janet Berry	1891-1894 and 1898-1906

Mixed School

J Robert Markham	1894-1898
George G Hague	1906-1924
Herbert C Marshall	1925-1938
John R Ward	1939-1948
George L Armitage	1948-1967
R Norman Lister	1968-1983
John M Brooke	1984-1997
Anthony R Berwick	1998-2003
Charles R V Woodbridge	2004-

2. Teaching Staff 1894-2019

The pre-1894 log books are missing so it is impossible to give the names of staff prior to then. Temporary and 'supply' staff are not included here.

TH Holmes	*	to	20. 4.1894
H Lister	*	to	1. 6.1894
A Ainsworth	1887(?)	to	31. 8.1895
H Tomlinson	1887(?)	to	31. 8.1895
Miss * Bairstow	*	to	25.10.1895
Miss Morton	*	to	24. 8.1894
Miss * Binns	1880(?)	to	30. 6.1898
Miss A Oates	1888	to	30.11.1904
Miss F Aspinall	1.12.1894	to	27. 7.1899
H H Schofield	25.10.1895	to	26. 2.1897
Miss E Kershaw	1.11.1895	to	4. 5.1897
Miss M A Allen	1. 3.1897	to	23. 7.1897
Miss M L Moorhouse	16. 6.1897	to	12.12.1897
Miss H Normanton	*	to	28. 2.1900
Miss E Clayton	1. 7.1898	to	20. 6.1900
Mrs J Turner	17. 8.1898	to	21. 8.1899
(née Flather) and	9. 1.1905	to	30. 6.1921

H Mitchell	10. 4.1899	to	21. 8.1899
Miss I Binns	2.10.1899	to	30. 8.1901
Mrs J Bottomley	21. 8.1899	to	29. 6.1900
Miss C Topham	26. 1.1900	to	30. 8.1901
Miss F Wells	10. 7.1900	to	30.10.1904
Miss B Kershaw	27. 8.1900	to	15. 2.1901
Miss F Garside	25. 2.1901	to	6. 2.1903
Miss I Cockcroft	2. 9.1901	to	* 1902
Miss J Hodgson	2. 9.1901	to	31. 5.1904
Miss E Bottomley	7. 4.1902	to	1.12.1905
Miss E Womersley	1. 7.1902	to	19.12.1947
Miss B Stead	2. 3.1903	to	24. 3.1910
Miss A Murgatroyd	14. 6.1904	to	30. 9.1904
Miss E Coates	27. 6.1905	to	20.12.1907
Miss * Sinkinson	10.11.1905	to	3. 7.1905
A Seed	9. 1.1905	to	31. 8.1905
Miss A Robinson	1.11.1905	to	31. 3.1916
Miss M Dalby	8. 1.1906	to	31. 7.1908
Miss H Walsh	2. 4.1906	to	31. 5.1918
Miss J Roper	7. 1.1908	to	25. 5.1928
Miss K H Kaye	31. 8.1908	to	28.10.1948
Mrs A M Thompson (née Hoyle)	9. 9.1909	to	30. 6.1926
Miss H Garside	1. 5.1916	to	31. 1.1917
Miss S Pohlman	5. 3.1917	to	31. 8.1921
Mrs L Hey	1. 8.1918	to	30. 9.1929
B Kendall	4. 7.1921	to	31. 3.1925
Mrs E Edwards	1.11.1921	to	28. 9.1928
(née Lee) and	1. 9.1943	to	18. 7.1960
Miss K Ackroyd	25. 8.1924	to	31. 9.1930
F Holdsworth	1. 7.1925	to	31. 8.1931
Miss P M Aspinall	1. 8.1928	to	18. 7.1960
Miss B Jessop	1.11.1928	to	31. 1.1933
Miss P H Sternwhite	18.12.1930	to	31.10.1939
T E H Scott	1.12.1931	to	31. 5.1934
Miss A G Robinson	1. 3.1933	to	31.10.1934
E Marsden	2. 7.1934	to	30. 9.1937
and	2.10.1939	to	8.12.1939
Miss M Ingham	* 1935	to	30. 9.1936
D Oates	8. 7.1935	to	29.10.1937
Miss M Sykes	2.11.1936	to	30.10.1938
R Norminton	1.10.1937	to	6. 1.1941
O James	1.11.1937	to	6. 1.1941
Miss M G Marsh	1.11.1938	to	31. 8.1939
Mrs K Murray	1.11.1939	to	21. 7.1966
Mrs E Smart	11.12.1939	to	17. 7.1953
Miss M Hemingway	27. 8.1940	to	31. 8.1949
Miss O M Ashworth	27. 8.1940	to	4. 8.1944
J Crossley	5. 1.1948	to	18. 7.1952
R N Lister	14. 3.1949	to	19.12.1953

B D Wildsmith	4. 9.1950	to	17. 7.1953
Mrs E D A Smith	4. 9.1950	to	20. 7.1951
Mrs W Inman	3. 9.1951	to	17. 4.1957
R A Lee	5. 1.1953	to	22. 7.1955
Mrs N Waud	31. 8.1953	to	21.12.1960
H Laycock (DHT)	11. 1.1954	to	19.12.1969
Miss R Sykes	6. 9.1954	to	18. 7.1960
P R Brearley	3. 9.1956	to	18.12.1959
Miss D Sutcliffe	1. 9.1958	to	18. 7.1960
D Shepherd	6. 1.1960	to	18. 7.1960
J M Brooke	5. 9.1960	to	5. 4.1966
Miss N M Attack	5. 9.1960	to	21. 7.1961
Mrs M Burkinshaw	5. 9.1960	to	21. 7.1961
Mrs D C Crossley	5. 9.1960	to	21.12.1960
A Naylor	5. 9.1960	to	20. 7.1962
Mrs S P Hepworth	17. 4.1961	to	21.12.1962
Mrs M Dewison	29. 5.1961	to	21.12.1961
Mrs E M Lancaster (née Nutton)	4. 9.1961	to	31.10.1963
Miss M E Gale	4. 9.1961	to	20. 7.1962
Mrs M A Smith	3. 9.1962	to	21.12.1962
D Lee	10. 9.1962	to	19. 7.1963
and	5. 9.1966	to	21. 7.1967
Mrs J M Hastings	7. 1.1963	to	17. 7.1964
D J Dobson	6. 5.1963	to	17. 7.1964
Mrs S M Smith	2. 9.1963	to	17. 7.1964
Mrs M E Morrison	2. 9.1963	to	25. 3.1964
Mrs M H Nuttall	9. 4.1964	to	17. 7.1969
Mrs M J Hudson (née Whitley)	2. 9.1964	to	31. 1.1975
G G Hudson	2. 9.1964	to	21.12.1966
Mrs M Macdowell	6. 1.1965	to	23. 7.1965
and	4. 1.1967	to	2. 7.1967
Miss C Coyle	6. 9.1965	to	21. 7.1966
J E Barker	20. 4.1966	to	21. 7.1966
Mrs J E Brooke (née Brook)	5. 9.1966	to	18. 7.1969
and	1. 9.1980	to	21. 7.1983
Mrs E M Gledhill (née Titley)	5. 9.1966	to	11. 6.1971
and	27. 9.1978	to	6. 4.1979
Miss S M Wade	4. 9.1967	to	19.12.1967
M A Tomlinson	4. 9.1967	to	19.12.1967
L Briggs	4. 9.1967	to	17. 7.1970
Mrs S Cawkwell	3. 1.1968	to	14. 7.1978
Mrs A W Scott (née Maude)	3. 1.1968	to	20.12.1968
Mrs J M O'Rourke (née Loxam)	6. 1.1969	to	31. 3.2005
Mrs B Carney	2. 9.1969	to	2.12.1974
and	5. 1.1976	to	15. 7.1976
Mrs C Styan (née Shield)	2. 9.1969	to	20.12.1974
C J Wood	2. 9.1969	to	21. 7.1972
Mrs J Lumb	2. 9.1969	to	24. 2.1973
Mrs M Whitaker	6. 9.1971	to	16. 7.1996

R Leeming (DHT)	2. 9.1970	to	21.12.1972
Miss J M Nobbs	2. 9.1970	to	12. 7.1995
Mrs E Wood (née Beaumont)	6. 9.1971	to	22.11.1974
Mrs C Jowitt	6. 9.1971	to	14. 7.1978
Miss J McPhail	13. 4.1972	to	12. 7.1991
Miss P Hartley	5. 1.1972	to	20. 7.1973
C Woods (DHT)	3. 1.1973	to	20.12.1991
D Gill	3. 1.1973	to	15. 7.1976
Mrs P Marshall	3. 1.1973	to	22.12.1989
C Heywood	26. 2.1973	to	18. 7.1975
Mrs A Kendall	6. 1.1975	to	22.12.1981
Mrs M E Bates	6. 1.1975	to	21. 3.1986
Mrs V A Deadman	6. 1.1975	to	12. 7.1994
R A Robinson	1. 2.1975	to	10. 4.1981
K Dearn	1. 9.1975	to	1. 4.1977
Miss S Parker	5. 1.1975	to	18. 7.1980
Mrs A M Hankinson	1. 9.1975	to	15. 7.1988
A Rhodes	31. 8.1976	to	13. 4.1984
Miss E Beeson	29. 8.1978	to	13. 7.1979
Mrs M Benn	28. 8.1979	to	18. 7.1980
Mrs M J Hoyle	1. 9.1980	to	19.12.1980
and	30. 8.1983	to	31. 8.2012
R G Kinghorn	5. 1.1981	to	11. 7.1990
Mrs J Rind	27. 4.1981	to	17. 7.1981
Mrs B Horsman	1. 1.1981	to	21. 3.1986
Mrs M I Ingleheart	31. 8.1982	to	31. 8.1998
D J G Rooke	30. 8.1983	to	313. 8.2018
Mrs J Davies	30. 8.1983	to	13. 7.1984
F H Ogden	28. 8.1984	to	31. 8.2003
Mrs L Bottomley	7. 4.1986	to	11. 7.1986
Mrs R Paxman	1. 9.1987	to	31. 8.2013
Mrs B D Thornton	1. 9.1987	to	15. 7.1988
and	30. 8.1989	to	10. 7.1992
Miss J E Binns	1. 9.1987	to	15. 7.1988
mrs J C Crick	30. 8.1988	to	14. 7.1989
Mrs J E Beaumont (née Beevers)	30. 8.1989	–	
Mrs E D Shields	30. 8.1989	to	31. 8.2010
Mrs S F Brown (Thomson)	8. 1.1990	to	31. 8.2006
Mrs B Mirams	30. 8.1990	to	10. 4.1992
Mrs S J Blackhurst (Keitch) (née Whipp)	30. 8.1990	–	
Miss N M Dunkley	30. 8.1990	to	10. 7.1992
Mrs J P Thomas	30. 8.1990	–	31. 8.2004
Mrs J Burchill	30. 8.1990	to	31.12.2005
T R C Freeman	30. 8.1990	to	12. 7.1995
Mrs J I Jenkins	30. 8.1990	to	10. 4.1992
Mrs R Brooke (née Hallam)	30. 8.1991	–	
Mrs C V MacDonald (DHT)	27. 8.1992	to	31. 8.2012
Mrs T A Richardson (née Churm)	30. 8.1994	to	31. 1.2003

Miss K A Rushby	5. 9.1995	to	31. 8.1999
A J Inns	5. 9.1995	to	31. 8.2000
Miss G R Stanford	5. 9.1995	to	29. 3.1996
Miss S M Fox	3. 9.1996	to	31. 8.1999
Miss J Asquith	1. 9.1998	to	1. 8.2002
Mrs K Cooper	11. 9.2000	to	31. 8.2003
Miss K A Bourne	1. 9.2000	–	
Mrs L Webb (née Brookes)	1. 5.2000	–	
Mrs T Brennan	1. 9.2001	to	31.12.2009
Mrs E Maycock	1. 9.2001	to	31.12.2003
Miss C Scott	1. 9.2002	to	31. 8.2008
Mrs C Kemp	1. 9.2002	to	31. 8.2003
Mrs K Dunkley (DHT from 2012)	3. 8.2003	–	
Mrs T Hodgson	3. 9.2003	to	31. 8.2018
Mrs L J Moss (née Mann)	1. 9.2004	–	
Mrs D Grice	4.4.2005	to	24. 5.2017
Mrs M McDonald (née Millar)	1. 9.2005	–	
Mrs G Gillespie (née Ormrod)	5. 1.2105	–	
Miss H Austin	1. 9.2005	to	31. 8.2006
Mrs H Wood	1. 1.2006	to	31. 8.2019
Miss M Nolan	1. 9.2007	to	31.12.2014
Mrs J A Ball (née McGinty)	7. 1.2008	–	
Mrs T Barrie	1. 9.2009	to	31. 8.2010
Miss A Wilson	1. 8.2009	to	31. 8.2010
Mrs A Sheldrake	14.12.2009	to	11.12.2010
Mrs R L Schoon	4. 1.2010	–	
S Day	1. 9.2010	to	31.12.2014
Mrs A Hustler	1. 9.2012	–	
Mrs E J Langhorn (née Alcock)	1. 9.2012	–	
C O Wildgust	1. 9.2015	–	
Mrs L J Dukes	1. 9.2016	–	
Miss R J Parkinson	3. 9.2018	–	
Mrs R R Rowlands	1. 9.2019	–	

* Dates or initials unknown
DHT - Deputy Headteacher

3. Caretakers from 1894

H Longbottom	-1902
F Bradley	1902-1913
H Harris	1913-1915
B Cross	1915-1942
Mrs M Cross	1942-1944
W J Berryman	1945-1949
J C Hill	1949-1961
W Haigh	1961-1967
S Whitley	1967-1970

G Robins	1970-1975
Mrs g Bland	1975-1979
B W Moore	1979-2016
R Brear	2017-2018
Mrs J Kershaw	2018-

4 Chair of Managers/Governors

Until Patrick Beeson succeeded David Wilding in 1993 it was common practice for the vicar to be chairman of the managing/governing body. Pat was followed by Stanley Coulton, David Hyatt, Richard Greenwood, Christine Stephenson and, currently, Richard Monro

Vicars whose incumbency embraced the period from the school's opening, and acted as chairman, are as follows:

William Gurney	1840
George Bagot	1869
Vivian R Lennard	1883
Alexander J Harrison	1888
N Lyndon Parkyn	1894
James R Hill	1897
Henry A Kennedy	1903
Richard P Whittington	1907
Charles L Hulbert	1911
Harold L Taylor	1914
Frank White	1955
Michael G S Whitcombe	1972
David Wilding	1979

Vicars who then just became ex-officio members of the governing body:

Robert S Cooper	1998
Peter Sutcliffe	2006
Kathryn Buck	2010

5. Present Staff

A list of the current staff as presented by the school in October 2019.

Mrs J Ball	Teacher
Mrs J Beaumont	Teacher
Mrs H Bell	Business Manager
Mrs S Blackhurst	Teacher
Miss K Bourne	Teacher
Mrs M. Brook	Classroom Support Assistant
Mrs R Brooke	Teacher
Miss N Brown	General Kitchen Assistant
Mrs A Brunkard	Reception Class Assistant
Mr C Cardy	General Kitchen Assistant

Miss P Clark	Higher Level Teaching Assistant
Mrs S Coldwell	Mid-day Supervisor/General Support Assistant
Mrs K Dewhirst	Mid-day Supervisor
Mrs L Dukes	Teacher
Mrs K Dunkley	Deputy Headteacher
Mrs A Edmondson	Reception Class Assistant
Mrs A Eliasz	Assistant Cook
Mrs D Ellis	Reception Class Assistant
Mrs E Field	Mid-day Supervisor/Cleaner
Mrs G Gillespire	Teacher
Mrs C Goddard	Mid-day Supervisor/Classroom Support
Mrs A Greenwood	Receptionist
Mrs G Gregg	General Kitchen Assistant/Cleaner
Mrs A Hemingway	General Special Education Needs
Mrs R Ho	Classroom Support Assistant/Mid-day Supervisor
Mrs A Hustler	Assistant Headteacher
Mrs J Jackson	Classroom Support Assistant
Mrs J Kershaw	Premises Supervisor
Mrs C Kinghorn	General Kitchen Assistant
Mrs E Langhorn	Teacher
Mrs M Laycock	Mid-day Supervisor//Better Reading Co-ordinator
Mrs M McDonald	Teacher
Mrs L Moss	Teacher
Mrs C Nicholl	Classroom Support Assistant
Mrs B O'Rourke	Administrator
Miss R Parkinson	Teacher
Mrs V Parkinson	Mid-day Supervisor
Ms A Rhodes	Mid-day Supervisor/Cleaner
Miss A Rollinson	Classroom Support Assistant
Mrs R Rowlands	Teacher
Mrs R Schoon	Teacher
Mrs C Stansfield	Higher Level Teaching Assistant/Cleaner
Mrs C Stephenson	Senior Mid-day Supervisor
Mrs J Stoker	Classroom Support Assistant
Mrs D Swift	Learning Mentor
Mrs K Thomas	Reception Class Assistant
Mr P Tyler	Head Chef
Mrs C Watson	Higher Level Teaching Assistant
Mrs V Webb	Teacher
Mrs T Whelan	Mid-day Supervisor
Mr C Wildgust	Teacher
Mrs J Wilson	Special Education Needs Support/ Classroom Support Assistant
Ms D Wood	Classroom Support Assistant
Mr C Woodbridge	Headteacher

A summary of sources consulted

Barnard, HC, *A Short History of English Education: 1760-1944* (University of London Press, 1947)

Brooke, John and Hudson, Geoffrey, *The Story of a School: Lightcliffe CE School,* (The School managers/governors, 1969/1987)

Cruickshank, Marjorie, *Church and State in English Education,* (Macmillan, 1963)

Horne, Bob and Brooke, John, *Village Voices,* (Lightcliffe and District Local History Society, 2007)

Horsfall Turner,J, *History of Brighouse, Rastrick and Hipperholme,* (Privately published, 1893)

Lightcliffe School records currently held by the school: logbooks, admission registers, governors (managers) minutes, photographs.

Maclure, J Stuart, *Educational Documents. England and Wales: 1816-1967,* (Chapman and Hall, 1965)

Murphy, James, *Church, State and Schools in Britain: 1860-1970* (Routledge and Kegan Paul, 1971)

Murray, Nicholas, *A life of Matthew Arnold,* (St Martin's Press,1997)

National Archives, *Lightcliffe School (listed under Hipperholme cum Brighouse Lightcliffe National School). 1894-1914.*(ED 21/20212)

Newspapers: *The Halifax Courier, The Halifax Guardian, The Brighouse (and Elland) Echo.*

Parish Records, Lightcliffe: *1665-2000,* WYAS, Wakefield. (WDP 47)

Parker, James, Illustrated Rambles from Hipperholme to Tong (Percy, Lund and Humphries, 1904)

Sturt, Mary, *The Education of the People,* (Routledge and Kegan Paul,1967)

Teachers' Registration Council Records.

Waterson, E and Meadows P, *The Lost Houses of the West RIding,* (Jill Raines, 1998)

Websites: *Ancestry and Find My Past.*

West Yorkshire Archive Service [WYAS] Calderdale: *1953-85, (File3318); 1965-72 (CMB D1/12/8/8. Box1599) and 1965-86 (CMB D1/12/1/37/1-2. Box 1523).* Wakefield: *(Within parish records, WDP47/Box 11)*

Index of people named in the main text

Endnote

Educating Three Generations

James Horne is pictured in the centre on the back row of Barbara Horsman's class in 1991. His father, Bob, who has written the book's *foreword* attended the school, as does George, James's son. There will have been many similar examples over the years of three or more generations who have attended the school.